The Bashful Lover by Philip Massinger

Philip Massinger was baptized at St. Thomas's in Salisbury on November 24th, 1583.

Massinger is described in his matriculation entry at St. Alban Hall, Oxford (1602), as the son of a gentleman. His father, who had also been educated there, was a member of parliament, and attached to the household of Henry Herbert, 2nd Earl of Pembroke. The Earl was later seen as a potential patron for Massinger.

He left Oxford in 1606 without a degree. His father had died in 1603, and accounts suggest that Massinger was left with no financial support this, together with rumours that he had converted to Catholicism, meant the next stage of his career needed to provide an income.

Massinger went to London to make his living as a dramatist, but he is only recorded as author some fifteen years later, when The Virgin Martyr (1621) is given as the work of Massinger and Thomas Dekker.

During those early years as a playwright he wrote for the Elizabethan stage entrepreneur, Philip Henslowe. It was a difficult existence. Poverty was always close and there was constant pleading for advance payments on forthcoming works merely to survive.

After Henslowe died in 1616 Massinger and John Fletcher began to write primarily for the King's Men and Massinger would write regularly for them until his death.

The tone of the dedications in later plays suggests evidence of his continued poverty. In the preface of The Maid of Honour (1632) he wrote, addressing Sir Francis Foljambe and Sir Thomas Bland: "I had not to this time subsisted, but that I was supported by your frequent courtesies and favours."

The prologue to The Guardian (1633) refers to two unsuccessful plays and two years of silence, when the author feared he had lost popular favour although, from the little evidence that survives, it also seems he had involved some of his plays with political characters which would have cast shadows upon England's alliances.

Philip Massinger died suddenly at his house near the Globe Theatre on March 17th, 1640. He was buried the next day in the churchyard of St. Saviour's, Southwark, on March 18th, 1640. In the entry in the parish register he is described as a "stranger," which, however, implies nothing more than that he belonged to another parish.

Index of Contents

DRAMATIS PERSONSAE

Gonzaga, Duke of Mantua.
Lorenzo, Duke of Tuscany.
Uberti, Prince of Parma.
Farneze, Cousin to Gonzaga.
Alonzo, the Ambassador, Nephew to Lorenzo.
Manfroy, a Lord of Mantua.
Octavio, formerly General to Gonzaga, but now in exile.
Gothrio, his Servant.
Galeazzo, a Milanese Prince, disguised under the name of Hortensio.
Julio, his Attendant.
Captains.
Milanese Ambassador.
Doctor.
Matilda, Daughter to Gonzaga.
Beatrice, her waiting Woman.
Maria, Daughter to Octavio, disguised as a Page, and called Ascanio.
Waiting Women.
Captains, Soldiers, Guard, Attendants, Page, &c.

SCENE: Partly in the City of Mantua, and Partly in the Dutchy.

PROLOGUE

This from our author, far from all offence
To abler writers, or the audience
Met here to judge his poem. He, by me,
Present; his service, with such modesty
As well becomes his "weakness. ' Tis no crime,
He hopes, as we do, in this curious time,
To be a little diffident, when, we are
To please so many with one bill of fare.
Let others, building on their merit, say
You're in the wrong, if you move not that way
Which they prescribe you; as you were bound to learn
Their maxims, but uncapable to discern
'Twixt truth and falsehood. Ours had rather be
Censured by some for too much obsequy,
Than tax'd of self opinion. If he hear
That his endeavours thrived, and did appear
Worthy your view, (though made so by your grace,
With some desert,) he, in another place,
Will thankfully report, one leaf of bays
Truly conferrd upon this work, will raise
More pleasure in him, you the givers free,
Than garlands ravish d from the virgin tree.

ACT I

SCENE I. Mantua. A Space Before the Palace

Enter **HORTENSIO** and **JULIO**.

JULIO
I dare not cross you, sir, but I would gladly
(Provided you allow it) render you
My personal attendance.

HORTENSIO
You shall better
Discharge the duty of an honest servant,
In following my instructions, which you have
Received already, than in questioning
What my intents are, or upon what motives

My stay's resolved in Mantua: believe me,
That servant overdoes, that's too officious;
And, in presuming to direct your master,
You argue him of weakness, and yourself
Of arrogance and impertinence.

JULIO
I have done, sir;
But what my ends are

HORTENSIO
Honest ones, I know it.
I have my bills of exchange, and all provisions,
Entrusted to you; you have shown yourself
Just and discreet, what would you more? and yet,
To satisfy in some part your curious care,
Hear this, and leave me. I desire to be
Obscured; and, as I have demean'd myself
These six months past in Mantua, I'll continue
Unnoted and unknown, and, at the best,
Appear no more than a gentleman, and a stranger,
That travels for his pleasure.

JULIO
With your pardon,
This hardly will hold weight, though I should swear it,
With your noble friends and brother.

HORTENSIO
You may tell them,
Since you will be my tutor, there's a rumour,
Almost cried up into a certainty.
Of wars with Florence, and that I am determined
To see the sen-ice: whatever I went forth,
Heaven prospering my intents, I would come home
A soldier, and a good one.

JULIO
Should you get
A captain's place, nay, colonel's, 'twould add little
To what you are; few of your rank will follow
That dangerous profession.

HORTENSIO
Tis the noblest,
And monarchs honour'd in it: but no more,
On my displeasure.

JULIO
Saints and angels guard you!

[Exit.

HORTENSIO
A war, indeed, is threaten'd, nav, expected,
From Florence; but it is 'gainst me already
Proclaim 'd in Mantua; I find it here,
No foreign, but intestine war: I have
Defied myself, in giving up my reason
A slave to passion, and am led captive
Before the battle's fought: I fainted, when
I only saw mine enemy, and yielded,
Before that I was charged; and, though defeated,
I dare not sue for mercy. Like Ixion,
I look on Juno, feel my heart turn cinders
With an invisible fire; and yet, should she
Deign to appear clothed in a various cloud,
The majesty of the substance is so sacred,
I durst not clasp the shadow. I behold her
With adoration, feast my eye, while all
My other senses starve; and, oft frequenting
The place which she makes happy with her presence,
I never yet had power with tongue or pen
To move her to compassion, or make known
What 'tis I languish for; yet I must gaze still,
Though it increase my flame: however, I
Much more than fear I am observed, and censured
For bold intrusion.

[Walks by.

[Enter **BEATRICE** and **ASCANIO**.

BEATRICE
Know you, boy, that gentleman?

ASCANIO
Who? monsieur Melancholy? hath not your honour
Mark'd him before?

BEATRICE
I have seen him often wait
About the princess' lodgings, but ne'er guess'd
What his designs were.

ASCANIO

No! what a sigh he breath'd now!
Many such will blow up the roof: en my small credit
There's gunpowder in them.

BEATRICE
How, crack! gunpowder?
He's flesh and blood, and devils only carry
Such roaring stuff about them: you cannot prove
He is or spirit or conjurer.

ASCANIO
That I grant,
But he's a lover, and that's as bad; their sighs
Are like petards, and blow all up.

BEATRICE
A lover!
I have been in love myself, but never found yet
That it could work such strange effects.

ASCANIO
True, madam,
In women it cannot; for when they miss the enjoying
Of their' full wishes, all their sighs and heigh-hoes,
At the worst, breed tympanies, and these are cured too
With a kiss or two of their saint, when he appears
Between a pair of sheets: but, with us men,
The case is otherwise.

BEATRICE
You will be breech 'd, boy,
For your physical maxims. But how are you assured,
He is a lover?

ASCANIO [Whispers]
Who, I? I know with whom too:
But that is to be whisper'd.

BEATRICE
How! the princess!
The unparallel'd Matilda! some proof of it-
I'll pay for my intelligence.

[Gives **ASCANIO** money.

ASCANIO
Let me kiss
Your honour's hand; 'twas ever fair, but now

Beyond comparison.

BEATRICE
I guess the reason;
A giving hand is still fair to the receiver.

ASCANIO
Your ladyship's in the right; but to the purpose.
He is my client, and pays his fees as duly
As ever usurer did, in a bad cause,
To his man of law; and yet I get, and take them
Both easily and honestly: all the service
I do him, is, to give him notice when
And where the princess will appear; and that
I hope's no treason. If you miss him, when
She goes to the vesper or the matins, hang me;
Or when she takes the air, be sure to find him
Near her coach, at her going forth, or coming back:
But if she walk, he's ravish 'd. I have seen him
Smell out her footing like a lime-hound, and nose it
From all the rest of her train.

BEATRICE
Yet I ne'er saw him
Present her a petition.

ASCANIO
Nor e'er shall:
He only sees her, sighs, and sacrifices
A tear or two then vanishes.

BEATRICE
'Tis most strange:
What a sad aspect he wears! but I'll make use oft.
The princess is much troubled with the threats
That come from Florence; I will bring her to him,
The novelty may afford her sport, and help
To purge deep melancholy. Boy, can you stay
Your client here for the third part of an hour?
I have some ends in't.

ASCANIO
Stay him, madam! fear not:
The present receipt of around sum of crowns,
And that will draw most gallants from their prayers,
Cannot drag him from me.

BEATRICE

See you do.

[Exit.

ASCANIO
Ne'er doubt me.
I'll put him out of his dream. Good morrow, signior.

HORTENSIO
My little friend, good morrow.
Hath the princess
Slept well to-night?

ASCANIO
I hear not from her women
One murmur to the contrary.

HORTENSIO
Heaven be praised for't!
Does she go to church this morning?

ASCANIO
Troth, I know not;
I keep no key of her devotion, signior.

HORTENSIO
Goes she abroad? pray tell me.

ASCANIO
'Tis thought rather,
She is resolv'd to keep her chamber.

HORTENSIO
Ah me!

ASCANIO
Why do you sigh? if that you have a business
To be dispatch'd in court, shew ready money,
You shall find those that will prefer it for you.

HORTENSIO
Business! can any man have business, but
To see her; then admire her, and pray for her,
She being composed of goodness? for myself,
I find it a degree of happiness
But to be near her, and I think I pay
A strict religious vow, when I behold her;
And that's all my ambition.

ASCANIO

I believe you:
Yet, she being absent, you may spend some hours
With profit and delight too. After dinner,
The duke gives audience to a rough ambassador,
Whom yet I never saw, nor heard his title,
Employ 'd from Florence; I'll help you to a place,
Where you shall see and hear all.

HORTENSIO

'Tis not worth
My observation.

ASCANIO

What think you of
An excellent comedy, to be presented
For his entertainment? he that penn'd it is
The poet of the time, and all the ladies,
(I mean the amorous and learned ones,)
Except the princess, will be there to grace it.

HORTENSIO

What's that to me? without her all is nothing;
The light that shines in court Cimmerian darkness;
I will to bed again, and there contemplate
On her perfections.

[Re-enter **BEATRICE** with **MATILDA**, and **TWO WAITING-WOMEN**.

ASCANIO

Stay, sir, see! the princess,
Beyond our hopes.

HORTENSIO

Take that.

[Gives him money.

As Moors salute
The rising sun with joyful superstition,
I could fall down and worship. O my heart!
Like Phoebe breaking through an envious cloud,
Or something which no simile can express,
She shews to me: a reverent fear, but blended
With wonder and amazement, does possess me.
Now glut thyself, my famish 'd eye!

BEATRICE
That 'she,
An't please your excellence.

1ST WOMAN
Observe his posture,
But with a quarter-look.

2ND WOMAN
Your eye fix'd on him,
Will breed astonishment.

MATILDA
A comely gentleman!
I would not question your relation, lady,
Yet faintly can believe it. How he eyes me!
Will he not speak?

BEATRICE
Your excellence hath deprived him
Of speech and motion.

MATILDA
'Tis most strange.

ASCANIO
These fits
Are usual with him.

MATILDA
Is it not, Ascanio,
A personated folly! or he a statue?
If it be, it is a masterpiece; for man
I cannot think him.

BEATRICE
For your sport, vouchsafe him
A little conference.

MATILDA
In compassion rather:
For should he love me, as you say, (though hopeless,)
It should not be return'd with scorn; that were
An inhumanity, which my birth nor honour
Could privilege, were they greater. Now I perceive
He has life and motion in him. To whom, lady,
Pays he that duty?

[**HORTENSIO**, bowing, offers to go off.

BEATRICE
Sans doubt, to yourself.

MATILDA
And whither goes he now?

ASCANIO
To his private lodging,
But to what end I know not; this is all
I ever noted in him.

MATILDA
Call him back:
In pity I stand bound to counsel him,
Howe'er I am denied, though I were willing,
To ease his sufferings.

ASCANIO
Signior! the princess
Commands you to attend her.

HORTENSIO [Returns]
How! the princess!
Am I betray'd?

ASCANIO
What a lump of flesh is this!
You are betray'd, sir, to a better fortune
Than you durst ever hope for. What a Tantalus
Do you make yourself! the flying fruit stays for you,
And the water that you long'd for, rising up
Above your lip, do you refuse to taste it?
Move faster, sluggish camel, or I'll thrust
This goad in your breech: had I such a promising beard,
I should need the reins, not spurs.

MATILDA
You may come nearer.
Why do you shake, sir? If I flatter not
Myself, there's no deformity about me,
Nor any part so monstrous, to beget
An ague in you.

HORTENSIO
It proceeds not, madam,
From guilt, but reverence.

MATILDA
I believe you, sir;
Have you a suit to me?

HORTENSIO
Your excellence
Is wondrous fair.

MATILDA
I thank your good opinion.

HORTENSIO
And I beseech you that I may have license
To kneel to you.

MATILDA
A suit I cannot cross.

HORTENSIO
I humbly thank your excellence.

[Kneels.

MATILDA
But what,
As you are prostrate on your knee before me,
Is your petition?

HORTENSIO
I have none, great princess.

MATILDA
Do you kneel for nothing?

HORTENSIO
Yes, I have a suit,
But such a one, as, if denied, will kill me.

MATILDA
Take comfort: it must be of some strange nature,
Unfitting you to ask, or me to grant,
If I refuse it.

HORTENSIO
It is, madam

MATILDA

Out with't.

HORTENSIO
That I may not offend you, this is all,
When I presume to look on you.

ASCANIO
A flat eunuch!
To look on her? I should desire myself
To move a little further.

MATILDA
Only that?

HORTENSIO
And I beseech you, madam, to believe
I never did yet with a wanton eye;
Or cherish one lascivious wish beyond it.

BEATRICE
You'll never make good courtier, or be
In grace with ladies.

1ST WOMAN
Or us waiting women,
If that be your nil ultra.

2ND WOMAN
He's no gentleman,
On my virginity, it is apparent:
My tailor has more boldness; nay, my shoe-maker
Will fumble a little further, he could not have
The length of my foot else.

MATILDA
Only to look on me!
Ends your ambition there?

HORTENSIO
It does, great lady,
And that confined too, and at fitting distance:
The fly that plays too near the flame burns in it.
As I behold the sun, the stars, the temples,
I look on you, and wish it were no sin
Should I adore you.

MATILDA
Come, there's something more in't;

And since that you will make a goddess of me,
As such a one I'll tell you, I desire not
The meanest altar raised up to mine honour
To be pull'd down; I can accept from you,
Be your condition ne'er so far beneath me,
One grain of incense with devotion offer'd,
Beyond all perfumes, or Sabsean spices,
By one that proudly thinks he merits in it:
I know you love me.

HORTENSIO
Next to heaven, madam,
And with as pure a zeal. That, we behold
With the eyes of contemplation, but can
Arrive no nearer to it in this life;
But when that is divorced, my soul shall serve yours,
And witness my affection.

MATILDA
Pray you, rise;
But wait my further pleasure,

[**HORTENSIO** rises and walks aside.

[Enter **FARNEZE** and **UBERTI**.

Farn, I'll present you,
And give you proof I am your friend, a true one;
And in my pleading for you, teach the age,
That calls, erroneously, friendship but a name,
It is a substance. Madam, I am bold
To trench so far upon your privacy,
As to desire my friend (let not that wrong him,
For he's a worthy one) may have the honour
To kiss your hand.

MATILDA
His own worth challenges
A greater favour.

FARNEZE
Your acknowledgment
Confirms it, madam. If you look on him
As he's built up a man, without addition
Of fortune's liberal favours, wealth or titles,
He doth deserve no usual entertainment:
But, as he is a prince, and for your service
Hath left fair Parma, that acknowledges

No other lord, and, uncompell'd, exposes
His person to the dangers of the war,
Ready to break in storms upon our heads;
In noble thankfulness you may vouchsafe him
Nearer respect, and such grace as may nourish,
Not kill, his amorous hopes.

MATILDA
Cousin, you know
I am not the disposer of myself,
The duke my father challenges that power:
Yet thus much I dare promise; prince Uberti
Shall find the seed of service that he sows,
Falls not on barren ground.

UBERTI
For this high favour
I am your creature, and profess I owe you
Whatever I call mine.

[They walk aside.

HORTENSIO
This great lord is
A suitor to the princess.

ASCANIO
True, he is so.

HORTENSIO
Fame gives him out too for a brave commander.

ASCANIO
And in it does him but deserved right;
The duke hath made him general of his horse,
On that assurance.

HORTENSIO
And the lord Farneze,
Pleads for him, as it seems.

ASCANIO
'Tis too apparent:
And, this consider'd, give me leave to ask
What hope have you, sir?

HORTENSIO
I may still look on her,

Howe'er he wear the garland.

ASCANIO
A thin diet,
And will not feed you fat, sir.

UBERTI
I rejoice,
Rare princess, that you are not to be won
By carpet-courtship, but the sword; with this
Steel pen I'll write on Florence' helm how much
I can, and dare do for you.

MATILDA
'Tis not question'd.
Some private business of mine own disposed of,
I'll meet you in the presence.

UBERTI
Ever your servant.

[Exeunt **UBERTI** and **FARNEZE**.

MATILDA
Now, sir, to you. You have observed, I doubt not,
For lovers are sharp-sighted, to what purpose
This prince solicits me; and yet I am not
So taken with his worth, but that I can
Vouchsafe you further parle. The first command
That I'll impose upon you, is to hear
And follow my good counsel: I am not
Offended that you love me, persist in it,
But love me virtuously; such love may spur you
To noble undertakings, which achieved,
Will raise you into name, preferment, honour:
For all which, though you ne'er enjoy my person,
(For that's impossible,) you are indebted
To your high aims: visit me when you please,
I do allow it, nor will blush to own you,
So you confine yourself to what you promise,
As my virtuous servant.

BEATRICE
Farewell, sir! you have
An unexpected cordial.

ASCANIO
May it work well!

[Exeunt all but **HORTENSIO**.

HORTENSIO
Your love yes, so she said, may spur you to
Brave undertakings: adding this, You may
Visit me when you please. Is this allow'd me.
And any act, within the power of man,
Impossible to be effected? no:
I wall break through all oppositions that
May stop me in my full career to honour:
And, borrowing strength to do, from her high favour,
Add something to Alcides' greatest labour.

[Exit.

SCENE II. The Same. A State-Room in the Palace

Enter **GONZAGA**, **UBERTI**, **FARNEZE**, **MANFROY**, and **ATTENDANTS**.

GONZAGA
This is your place; and, were it in our power,

[Leads **UBERTI** to the state.

You should have greater honour, prince of Parma;
The rest know theirs. Let some attend with care
On the ambassador, and let my daughter
Be present at his audience.

[Exeunt **ATTENDANTS**.

Reach a chair,
We'll do all fit respects; and, pray you, put on
Your milder looks, you are in a place where frowns
Are no prevailing agents. [To **UBERTI**.

[Enter at one door **ALONZO** and **ATTENDANTS**: **MATILDA**, **BEATRICE ASCANIO**, **HORTENSIO**, and
WAITING-WOMEN, at the other.

ASCANIO
I have seen
More than a wolf, a Gorgon!

[Swoons.

GONZAGA
What's the matter?

MATILDA
A page of mine is fallen into a swoon;
Look to him carefully.

[**ASCANIO** is carried out.

GONZAGA
Now, when you please,
The cause that brought you hither?

ALONSO
The protraction
Of my dispatch forgotten, from Lorenzo,
The Tuscan duke, thus much to you,
Gonzaga,
The duke of Mantua. By me, his nephew,
He does salute you fairly, and entreats
(A word not suitable to his power and greatness)
You would consent to tender that which he,
Unwilling), must force, if contradicted.
Ambition, in a private man a vice,
Is, in a prince, the virtue.

GONZAGA
To the purpose;
These ambages are impertinent.

ALONSO
He demands
The fair Matilda, for I dare not take
From her perfections, in a noble way;
And in creating her the comfort of
His royal bed, to raise her to a height
Her flattering hopes could not aspire, where she
With wonder shall be gazed upon, and live
The envy of her sex.

GONZAGA
Suppose this granted.

UBERTI
Or, if denied, what follows?

ALONSO
Present war,

With all extremities the conqueror can
Inflict upon the vanquish 'd.

UBERTI
Grant me license
To answer this defiance. What intelligence
Holds your proud master with the will of heaven,
That, ere the uncertain die of war be thrown,
He dares assure himself the victory?
Are his unjust invading arms of fire?
Or those we put on in defence of right,
Like chaff, to be consumed in the encounter?
I look on your dimensions, and find not
Mine own' of lesser size; the blood that fills
My veins, as hot as yours; my sword as sharp,
My nerves of equal strength, my heart as good;
And, confident we have the better cause,
Why should we fear the trial?

FARNEZE
You presume
You are superior in numbers; we
Lay hold upon the surest anchor, virtue;
Which, when the tempest of the war roars loudest,
Must prove a strong protection.

GONZAGA
Two main reasons
(Seconding those you have already heard)
Give us encouragement; the duty that
I owe my mother-country, and the love
Descending to my daughter. For the first,
Should I betray her liberty, I deserv'd
To have my name with infamy razed from
The catalogue of good princes; and I should
Unnaturally forget I am a father,
If, like a Tartar, or for fear or profit,
I should consign her, as a bondwoman,
To be disposed of at another's pleasure;
Her own consent or favour never sued for,
And mine by force exacted. No, Alonzo,
She is my only child, my heir; and, if
A father's eyes deceive me not, the hand
Of prodigal nature hath given so much to her,
As, in the former ages, kings would rise up
In her defence, and make her cause their quarrel:
Nor can she, if that any spark remain
To kindle a desire to be possess'd

Of such a beauty, in our time, want swords
To guard it safe from violence.

HORTENSIO
I must speak,
Or I shall burst; now to be silent were
A kind of blasphemy: if such purity,
Such innocence, an abstract of perfection,
The soul of beauty, virtue, in a word,
A temple of things sacred, should groan under
The burthen of oppression, we might
Accuse the saints, and tax the Powers above us
Of negligence or injustice. Pardon, sir,
A stranger's boldness, and in your mercy call it
True zeal, not rudeness. In a cause like this,
The husbandman would change his ploughing-irons
To weapons of defence, and leave the earth
Untill'd, although a general dearth should follow:
The student would forswear his book, the lawyer
Put off his thriving gown, and, without pay,
Conclude this cause is to be fought, not pleaded.
The women will turn Amazons, as their sex
In her were wrong'd; and boys write down their names
In the muster-book for soldiers.

GONZAGA
Take my hand:
Whate'er you are, I thank you. How are you call'd?

HORTENSIO
Hortensio, a Milanese.

GONZAGA
I wish
Mantua had many such. My lord ambassador,
Some privacy, if you please; Manfroy, you may
Partake it, and advise us.

[They walk aside.

UBERTI
Do you know, friend,
What this man is, or of what country?

FARNEZE
Neither.

UBERTI

I'll question him myself. What are you, sir?

HORTENSIO
A gentleman.

UBERTI
But if there be gradation
In gentry, as the heralds say, you have
Been over-bold in the presence of your betters.

HORTENSIO
My betters, sir!

UBERTI
Your betters. As I take it,
You are no prince.

HORTENSIO
'Tis fortune's gift you were born one;
I have not heard that glorious title crowns you,
As a reward of virtue: it may be,
The first of your house deserv'd it; yet his merits
You can but faintly call your own.

MATILDA
Well answer'd.

UBERTI
You come up to me.

HORTENSIO
I would not turn my back,
If you were the duke of Florence, though you charged me
I' the head of your troops.

UBERTI
Tell me in gentler language,
Your passionate speech induces me to think so,
Do you love the princess?

HORTENSIO
Were you mine enemy,
Your foot upon my breast, sword at my throat,
Even then I would profess it. The ascent
To the height of honour is by arts or arms
And if such an unequall'd prize might fall
On him that did deserve best in defence
Of this rare princess in the day of battle,

I should lead you a way would make your greatness
Sweat drops of blood to follow.

UBERTI
Can your excellence
Hear this without rebuke from one unknown?
Is he a rival for a prince?

MATILDA
My lord,
You take that liberty I never gave you.
In justice you should give encouragement
To him, or any man, that freely offers
His life to do me service, not deter him;
I give no suffrage to it. Grant he loves me,
As he professes, how are you wrong'd in it?
Would you have all men hate me but yourself?
No more of this, I pray you: if this gentleman
Fight for my freedom, in a fit proportion
To his desert and quality, I can
And will reward him; yet give you no cause
Of jealousy or envy.

HORTENSIO
Heavenly lady!

GONZAGA
No peace but on such poor and base conditions!
We will not buy it at that rate: return
This answer to your master: Though we wish'd
To hold fair quarter with him, on such terms
As honour would give way to, we are not
So thunderstruck with the loud voice of war,
As to acknowledge him our lord before
His sword hath made us vassals: we long since
Have had intelligence of the unjust gripe
He purposed to lay on us; neither are we
So unprovided as you think, my lord;
He shall not need so seek us; we will meet him,
And prove the fortune of a day, perhaps
Sooner than he expects.

ALONSO
And find repentance,
When 'tis too late. Farewell.

[Exit with **FARNEZE**.

GONZAGA

No, my Matilda,
We must not part so. Beasts and birds of prey,
To their last gasp, defend their brood; and Florence,
Over thy father's breast shall march up to thee,
Before he force affection. The arms
That thou must put on for us and thyself,
Are prayers and pure devotion, which will
Be heard, Matilda, Manfroy, to your trust
We do give up the city, and my daughter;
On both keep a strong guard No tears, they are ominous.
O my Octavio, my tried Octavio,
In all my dangers! now I want thy service,
In passion recompensed with banishment.
Error of princes, who hate virtue when
She's present with us, and in vain admire her
When she is absent! 'tis too late to think on't.
The wish 'd-for time is come, princely Uberti,
To shew your valour; friends, being to do, not talk,
All rhetoric is fruitless, only this,
Fate cannot rob you of deserv'd applause,
Whether you win or lose in such a cause.

[Exeunt.

ACT II

SCENE I. Mantua. A Room in the Palace

Enter **MATILDA, BEATRICE**, and **WAITING-WOMEN**.

MATILDA

No matter for the ring I ask'd you for.
The boy not to be found?

BEATRICE

Nor heard of, madam.

1ST WOMAN

He hath been sought and search'd for, house by house,
Nay, every nook of the city, but to no purpose.

2ND WOMAN

And how he should escape hence, the lord Manfroy
Being so vigilant o'er the guards, appears
A thing impossible.

MATILDA
I never saw him,
Since he swoon'd in the presence, when my father
Gave audience to the ambassador: but I feel
A sad miss of him; on any slight occasion,
He would find out such pretty arguments
To make me sport, and with such witty sweetness
Deliver his opinion, that I must
Ingenuously confess his harmless mirth
When I was most oppress'd with care, wrought more
In the removing oft, than music on me.

BEATRICE
An't please your excellence, I have observed him
Waggishly witty; yet, sometimes, on the sudden,
He would be very pensive; and then talk
So feelingly of love, as if he had
Tasted the bitter sweets oft.

1ST WOMAN
He would tell, too,
A pretty tale of a sister, that had been
Deceived by her sweetheart; and then, weeping, swear
He wonder'd how men could be false.

2ND WOMAN
And that
When he was a knight, he'd be the ladies' champion,
And travel o'er the world to kill such lovers,
As durst play false with their mistresses.

MATILDA
I am sure
I want his company.

[Enter **MANFROY**.

MANFROY
There are letters, madam,
In post come from the duke; but I am charged,
By the careful bringer, not to open them
But in your presence.

MATILDA
Heaven preserve my father!
Good news, an't be thy will! '

MANFROY
Patience must arm you
Against what's ill.

MATILDA
I'll hear them in my cabinet.

[Exeunt.

SCENE II. The Dutchy of Mantua. Gonzaga's Camp

Enter **HORTENSIO** and **ASCANIO**.

HORTENSIO
Why have you left the safety of the city,
And service of the princess, to partake
The dangers of the camp? and at a time too
When the armies are in view, and every minute
The dreadful charge expected?

ASCANIO
You appear
So far beyond yourself, as you are now,
Arm'd like a soldier, (though I grant your presence
Was ever gracious,) that I grow enamour'd
Of the profession: in the horror of it,
There is a kind of majesty.

HORTENSIO
But too heavy
To sit on thy soft shoulders, youth; retire
To the duke's tent, that's guarded.

ASCANIO
Sir, I come
To serve you; knight-adventurers are allow'd
Their pages, and I bring a will that shall
Supply my want of power.

HORTENSIO
To serve me, boy!
I wish, believe it, that 'twere in my nerves
To do thee any service; and thou shalt,
If I survive the fortune of this day,
Be satisfied I am serious.

ASCANIO
I am not
To be put off so, sir. Since you do neglect
My offer'd duty, I must use the power
I bring along with me, that may command you:
You have seen this ring

HORTENSIO
Made rich by being worn
Upon the princess' finger.

ASCANIO
'Tis a favour
To you, by me sent from her: view it better;
But why coy to receive it?

HORTENSIO
I am unworthy
Of such a blessing, I have done nothing yet
That may deserve it; no commander's blood
Of the adverse party hath yet died my sword
Drawn out in her defence. I must not take it.
This were a triumph for me when I had
Made Florence' duke my prisoner, and compell'd him
To kneel for mercy at her feet.

ASCANIO
'Twas sent, sir,
To put you in mind whose cause it is you fight for;
And, as I am her creature, to revenge
A wrong to me done.

HORTENSIO
By what man?

ASCANIO
Alonzo.

HORTENSIO
The ambassador?

ASCANIO
The same.

HORTENSIO
Let it suffice.
I know him by his armour and his horse;
And if we meet

[Trumpets sound.

I am cut off, the alarum
Commands me hence: sweet youth, fall off.

ASCANIO
I must not;
You are too noble to receive a wound
Upon your back, and, following close behind you,
I am secure; though I could wish my bosom
Were your defence.

HORTENSIO
Thy kindness will undo thee.

[Exeunt.

SCENE III. The Same. Lorenzo's Camp

Enter **LORENZO**, **ALONZO**, **PISANO**, and **MARTINO**.

LORENZO
We'll charge the main battalia, fall you
Upon the van preserve your troops entire,
To force the rear: he dies that breaks his ranks,
Till all be ours, and sure.

PISANO
'Tis so proclaim'd.

[Exeunt.

[Fighting and alarum. Enter **HORTENSIO**, **ASCANIO**, and **ALONZO**.

HORTENSIO
Tis he, Ascanio: Stand!

ALONSO
I never shunn'd
A single opposition; but tell me
Why, in the battle, of all men, thou hast
Made choice of me?

HORTENSIO
Look on this youth; his cause

Sits on my sword.

ALONSO
I know him not.

HORTENSIO
I'll help
Your memory.

[They fight.

ASCANIO
What have I done? I am doubtful
To whom to wish the victory; for, still
My resolution wavering, I so love
The enemy that wrong'd me, that I cannot,
Without repentance, wish success to him
That seeks to do me right.

[**ALONZO** falls.

Alas, he's fall'n!
As you are gentle, hold, sir! or, if I want
Power to persuade so far, I conjure you
By her loved name I am sent from.

HORTENSIO
Tis a charm
Too strong to be resisted: he is yours.
Yet, why you should make suit to save that life
Which you so late desired should be cut off,
For injuries received, begets my wonder.

ASCANIO
Alas! we foolish, spleenful boys would have
We know not what; I have some private reasons,
But now not to be told.

HORTENSIO
Shall I take him prisoner?

ASCANIO
By no means, sir; I will not save his life,
To rob him of his honour: when you give,
Give not by halves. One short word, and I
follow.

[Exit **HORTENSIO**.

My lord Alonzo, if you have received
A benefit, and would know to whom you owe it,
Remember what your entertainment was
At old Octavio's house, one you call'd friend,
And how you did return it.

[Exit.

ALONSO
I remember
I did not well; but it is now no time
To think upon't: my wounded honour calls
For reparation, I must quench my fury
For this disgrace, in blood, and some shall
smart for't.

[Exit.

SCENE IV. The Same. A Forest

Alarum continued. Enter **UBERTI**, and **FARNEZE** wounded.

FARNEZE
O prince Uberti, valour cannot save us;
The body of our army's pierced and broken,
The wings are routed, and our scatter 'd troops
Not to be rallied up.

UBERTI
'Tis yet some comfort,
The enemy must say we were not wanting
In courage or direction; and we may
Accuse the Powers above as partial, when
A good cause, well defended too, must suffer
For want of fortune.

FARNEZE
All is lost; the duke
Too far engaged, I fear, to be brought off:
Three times I did attempt his rescue, but
With odds was beaten back; only the stranger,
I speak it to my shame, still follow 'd him,
Cutting his way; but 'tis beyond my hopes,
That either should return.

UBERTI

That noble stranger,
Whom I, in my proud vanity of greatness,
As one unknown contemn'd, when I was thrown
Out of my saddle by the great duke's lance,
Horsed me again, in spite of all that made
Resistance; and then whisper'd in mine ear,
Fight bravely, prince Uberti, there's no way else.
To the fair Matilda's favour.

FARNEZE

'Twas done nobly.

UBERTI

In you, my bosom-friend, I had call'd it noble:
But such a courtesy from a rival merits
The highest attribute.

[Enter **HORTENSIO** and **GONZAGA**.

FARNEZE

Stand on your guard;
We are pursued.

UBERTI

Preserv d! wonder on wonder.

FARNEZE

The duke in safety!

GONZAGA

Pay your thanks, Farneze,
To this brave man, if I may call him so,
Whose acts were more than human. If thou art
My better angel, from my infancy
Design'd to guard me, like thyself appear,
For sure thou'rt more than mortal.

HORTENSIO

No, great sir,
A weak and sinful man; though I have done you
Some prosperous service that hath found your favour,
I am lost to myself: but lose not you
The offer'd opportunity to delude'
The hot-pursuing enemy; these woods,
Nor the dark veil of night, cannot conceal you,
If you dwell long here. You may rise again;
But I am fallen for ever.

FARNEZE
Rather borne up
To the supreme sphere of honour.

UBERTI
I confess
My life your gift.

GONZAGA
My liberty.

UBERTI
You have snatch'd
The wreath of conquest from the victor's head,
And do alone, in scorn of Lorenzo's fortune,.
Though we are slaved, by true heroic valour
Deserve a triumph.

GONZAGA
From whence then proceeds
This poor dejection?

HORTENSIO
In one suit I'll tell you,
Which I beseech you grant: I loved your daughter,
But how? as beggars in their wounded fancy,
Hope to be monarchs: I long languished for her,
But did receive no cordial, but what
Despair, my rough physician, prescribed me.
A length her goodness and compassion found it;
And, whereas I expected, and with reason,
The distance and disparity consider'd
Between her birth and mine, she would contemn me,
The princess gave me comfort.

GONZAGA
In what measure?

HORTENSIO
She did admit me for her knight and servant,
And spurr'd me to do something in this battle,
Fought for her liberty, that might not blemish
So fair a favour.

GONZAGA
This you have perform 'd,
To the height of admiration.

UBERTI
I subscribe to't,
That am your rival.

HORTENSIO
You are charitable:
But how short of my hopes, nay, the assurance
Of those achievements which my love and youth
Already held accomplish'd, this day's fortune
Must sadly answer. What I did, she gave me
The strength to do; her piety preserved
Her father, and her gratitude for the dangers
You threw yourself into for her defence,
Protected you by me her instrument:
But when I came to strike in mine own cause,
And to do something so remarkable,
That should at my return command her thanks
And gracious entertainment, then, alas!
I fainted like a coward. I made a vow, too,
(And it is register'd.) ne'er to presume
To come into her presence, if I brought not
Her fears and dangers bound in letters to her,
Which now's impossible. Hark! the enemy
Makes his approaches: save yourselves this only
Deliver to her sweetness; I have done
My poor endeavours, and pray her not repent
Her goodness to me. May you live to serve her,
This loss recover 'd, with a happier fate!
And make use of this sword: arms I abjure,
And conversation of men; I'll seek out
Some unfrequented cave, and die love's martyr.

[Exit hastily.

GONZAGA
Follow him.

UBERTI
'Tis in vain; his nimble feet
Have borne him from my sight.

GONZAGA
I suffer for him.

FARNEZE
We share in it; but must not, sir, forget
Your means of safety.

UBERTI

In the war I have served you,
And to the death will follow you.

GONZAGA

'Tis not fit,
We must divide ourselves. My daughter
If I retain yet
A sovereign's power o'er thee, or friend's with you,
Do, and dispute not; by my example change
Your habits: as I thus put off my purple,
Ambition dies; this garment of a shepherd,
Left here by chance, will serve; in lieu of it,
I leave this to the owner. Raise new forces,
And meet me at St. Leo's fort; my daughter,
As I commanded Manfroy, there will meet us.
The city cannot hold out, we must part:
Farewell, thy hand.

FARNEZE

You still shall have my heart.

[Exeunt.

SCENE V. The Same. Another Part of the Forest

Enter **LORENZO, ALONZO, PISANO, MARTINO, CAPTAINS**, and **SOLDIERS**.

LORENZO

The day is ours, though it cost dear; yet 'tis not
Enough to get a victory, if we lose
The true use of it. We have hitherto
Held back your forward swords, and in our fear
Of ambushes, deferr'd the wish'd reward
Due to your bloody toil: but now give freedom,
Nay, license to your fury and revenge;
Now glut yourselves with prey; let not the night,
Nor these thick woods, give sanctuary to
The fear-struck hares, our enemies: fire these trees,
And force the wretches to forsake their holes,
And offer their scorch'd bodies to your swords,
Or burn them as a sacrifice to your angers.
Who brings Gonzaga's head, or takes him prisoner,
(Which I incline to rather, that he may
Be sensible of those tortures, which I vow

To inflict upon him for denial of
His daughter to curbed,) shall have a blank,
With our hand and signet made authentical,
In which he may write down himself, what wealth
Or honours he desires.

ALONSO
The great duke's will
Shall be obey'd.

PISANO
Put it in execution.

MARTINO
Begirt the wood, and fire it.

SOLDIER
Follow, follow!

[Exeunt.

SCENE VI. The Same. Another Part of the Same

Enter **FARNEZE**, disguised as a Florentine Soldier.

FARNEZE
Uberti, prince Uberti! O my friend,
Dearer than life! I have lost thee. Cruel fortune,
Unsatisfied with our sufferings! we no sooner
Were parted from the duke, and e'en then ready
To take a mutual farewell, when a troop
Of the enemy's horse fell on us; we were forced
To take the woods again, but, in our flight,
Their hot pursuit divided us: we had been happy
If we had died together. To survive him,
To me is worse than death; and therefore should not
Embrace the means of my escape, though offer'd.
When nature gave us life she gave a burthen,
But at our pleasure not to be cast off,
Though weary of it; and my reason prompts me,
This habit of a Florentine, which I took
From a dying soldier, may keep me unknown,
Till opportunity mark me out a way
For flight, and with security.

[Enter **UBERTI**.

UBERTI

Was there ever
Such a night of horror?

FARNEZE

My friend's voice! I now
In part forgive thee, fortune.

UBERTI

The wood flames,
The bloody sword devours all that it meets,
And death in several shapes rides here in triumph.
I am like a stag closed in a toil, my life,
As soon as found, the cruel huntsman's prey:
Why fliest thou, then, what is inevitable?
Better to fall with manly wounds before
Thy cruel enemy, than survive thine honour:
And yet to charge him, and die unrevenged,
Mere desperation.

FARNEZE

Heroic spirit!

UBERTI

Mine own life I contemn, and would not save it
But for the future service of the duke,
And safety of his daughter; having means,
If I escape, to raise a second army;
And, what is nearest to me, to enjoy
My friend Farneze.

FARNEZE

I am still his care.

UBERTI

What shall I do? if I call loud, the foe
That hath begirt the wood, will hear the sound.
Shall I return by the same path? I cannot,
The darkness of the night conceals it from me;
Something I must resolve.

FARNEZE

Let friendship rouse
Thy sleeping soul, Farneze: wilt thou suffer
Thy friend, a prince, nay, one that may set free
Thy captived country, perish, when 'tis in
Thy power, with this disguise, to save his life?

Thou hast lived too long, therefore resolve to die;
Thou hast seen thy country ruin'd, and thy master
Compell'd to shameful flight; the fields and woods
Strew 'd o'er with carcasses of thy fellow soldiers:
The miseries thou art fallen in, and before
Thy eyes the horror of this place, and thousand
Calamities to come; and after all these,
Can any hope remain? shake off delays:
Dost thou doubt yet? To save a citizen,
The conquering Roman in a general
Esteem'd the highest honour: can it be then
Inglorious to preserve a prince? thy friend?
Uberti, prince Uberti! [Aloud] use this means
Of thy escape;

[Pulls off his Florentine uniform, and casts it before **UBERTI**.

—conceal'd in this, thou mayst
Pass through the enemy's guards: the time denies
Longer discourse; thou hast a noble end,
Live, therefore, mindful of thy dying friend.

[Exit.

UBERTI
Farneze, stay thy hasty steps!
Farneze!
Thy friend Uberti calls thee: 'tis in vain;
He's gone to death an innocent, and makes life,
The benefit he confers on me, my guilt.
Thou art too covetous of another's safety,
Too prodigal and careless of thine own.
'Tis a deceit in friendship to enjoin me
To put this garment on, and live, that he
May have alone the honour to die nobly.
O cruel piety, in our equal danger
To rob thyself of that thou giv'st thy friend!
It must not be; I will restore his gift,
And die before him. How? where shall I find him?
Thou art o'ercome in friendship; yield,
Uberti,
To the extremity of the time, and live:
A heavy ransome! but it must be paid.
I will put on this habit: pitying heaven,
As it loves goodness, may protect my friend,
And give me means to satisfy the debt
I stand engaged for; if not, pale despair,
I dare thy worst; thou canst but bid me die,

And so much I'll force from an enemy.

[Exit.

Enter **ALONZO** and **PISANO**, with **FARNEZE** bound; **SOLDIERS** with torches, Farneze 's sword in one of the **SOLDIER'S** hands.

ALONSO
I know him, he's a man of ransome.

PISANO
True;
But if he live, 'tis to be paid to me.

ALONSO
I forced him to the woods.

PISANO
But my art found him;
Nor will I brook a partner in the prey
My fortune gave me.

ALONSO
Render him, or expect
The point of this.

PISANO
Were it lightning, I would meet it,
Rather than be outbraved.

ALONSO
I thus decide
The difference.

PISANO
My sword shall plead my title.

[They fight.

[Enter **LORENZO, MARTINO, CAPTAINS**, and **ATTENDANTS**.

LORENZO
Ha! where learn'd you this discipline? my commanders
Opposed 'gainst one another! what blind fury

Brings forth this brawl? Alonzo and Pisano
At bloody difference! hold, or I tilt
At both as enemies. Now speak; how grew
This strange division?

PISANO
Against all right,
By force Alonzo strives to reap the harvest
Sown by my labour.

ALONSO
Sir, this is my prisoner,
The purchase of my sword, which proud
Pisano,
That hath no interest in him, would take from me.

PISANO
Did not the presence of the duke forbid me,
I would say

ALONSO
What?

PISANO
Tis false.

LORENZO
Before my face!
Keep them asunder. And was this the cause
Of such a mortal quarrel, this the base
To raise your fury on? the ties of blood,
Of fellowship in arms, respect, obedience
To me, your prince and general, no more
Prevailing on you? this a price for which
You would betray our victory, or wound
Your reputation with mutinies,
Forgetful of yourselves, allegiance, honour?
This is a course to throw us headlong down
From that proud height of empire, upon which
We were securely seated. Shall division
O'erturn what concord built? if you desire
To bathe your swords in blood, the enemy
Still flies before you: would you have spoil? the country
Lies open to you. O unheard-of madness!
What greater mischief could Gonzaga wish us,
Than you pluck on our heads? no, my brave leaders,
Let unity dwell in our tents, and discord
Be banis'h'd to our enemies.

ALONSO
Take the prisoner,
I do give up my title.

PISANO
I desire
Your friendship, and will buy it; he is yours.

[They embrace.

ALONSO
No man's a faithful judge in his own cause;
Let the duke determine of him: we are friends, sir.

LORENZO
Shew it in emulation to o'ertake
The flying foe; this cursed wretch disposed of,
With our whole strength we'll follow.

[Exeunt **ALONZO** and **PISANO** embracing.

FARNEZE
Death at length
Will set a period to calamity:
I see it in this tyrant's frowns haste to me.

[Enter **UBERTI**, habited like a Florentine Soldier, and mixes with the rest.

LORENZO
Thou machine of this mischief, look to feel
Whate'er the wrath of an incensed prince
Can pour upon thee: with thy blood I'll quench
(But drawn forth slowly) the invisible flames
Of discord by thy charms first fetch'd from hell,
Then forced into the breasts of my commanders.
Bring forth the tortures.

UBERTI
Hear, victorious duke,
The story of my miserable fortune,
Of which this villain (by your sacred tongue
Condemned to die) was the immediate cause:
And, if my humble suit have justice in it,
Vouchsafe to grant it.

LORENZO
Soldier, be brief, our anger

Can brook no long delay.

UBERTI
I am the last
Of three sons, by one father got, and train'd up
With his best care, for service in your wars:
My father died under his fatal hand,
And two of my poor brothers. Now I hear,
Or fancy, wounded by my grief, deludes me,
Their pale and mangled ghosts crying for vengeance
On perjury and murder. Thus the case stood:
My father, (on whose face he durst not look
In equal mart,) by his fraud circumvented,
Became his captive; we, his sons, lamenting
Our old sire's hard condition, freely offer'd
Our utmost for his ransome: that refused,
The subtile tyrant, for his cruel ends,
Conceiving that our piety might ensnare us,
Proposed my father's head to be redeem'd,
If two of us would yield ourselves his slaves.
We, upon any terms, resolved to save him,
Though with the loss of life which he gave to us,
With an undaunted constancy drew lots
(For each of us contended to be one)
Who should preserve our father; I was exempted,
But to my more affliction. My brothers
Deliver'd up, the perjured homicide,
Laughing in scorn, and by his hoary locks
Pulling my wretched father on his knees,
Said, Thus receive the father you have ransomed!
And instantly struck off his head.

LORENZO
Most barbarous!

FARNEZE
I never saw this man.

LORENZO
One murmur more,
I'll have thy tongue pull'd out. Proceed.

UBERTI
Conceive, sir,
How thunderstruck we stood, being made spectators
Of such an unexpected tragedy:
Yet this was a beginning, not an end
To his in'ended cruelty; for, pursuing

Such a revenge as no Hyrcanian tigress,
Robb'd of her whelps, durst aim at, in a moment,
Treading upon my father's trunk, he cut off
My pious brothers' heads, and threw them at me.
Oh, what a spectacle was this! what mountain
Of sorrow overwhelm'd me! my poor heart-strings,
As tenter 'd by his tyranny, crack'd; my knees
Beating 'gainst one another, groans and tears
Blended together follow'd; not one passion
Calamity ever yet express'd, forgotten.
Now, mighty sir, (bathing your feet with tears,)
Your suppliant's suit is, that he may have leave,
With any cruelty revenge can fancy,
To sacrifice this monster, to appease
My father's ghost, and brothers'.

LORENZO
Thou hast obtain'd it:
Choose any torture, let the memory
Of what thy father and thy brothers suffer'd,
Make thee ingenious in it; such a one,
As Phalaris would wish to be call'd his.
Martino, guarded with your soldiers, see
The execution done; but bring his head,
On forfeiture of your own, to us: our presence
Long since was elsewhere look'd for.

[Exit, with **CAPTAINS** and **ATTENDANTS**.

MARTINO
Soldier, to work;
Take any way thou wilt for thy revenge,
Provided that he die: his body's thine,
But I must have his head.

UBERTI
I have already
Concluded of the manner. O just heaven,
The instrument I wish'd for ofter'd me!

MARTINO
Why art thou rapt thus?

UBERTI
In this soldier's hand
I see the murderer's own sword, I know it;
Yes, this is it by which my father and
My brothers were beheaded: noble captain,

Command it to my hand.

[Takes Farneze's sword from the **SOLDIER**.

Stand forth and tremble!
This weapon, of late drunk with innocent blood,
Shall now carouse thine own: pray, if thou canst,
For, though the world shall not redeem thy body,
I would not kill thy soul.

FARNEZE
Canst thou believe
There is a heaven, or hell, or soul? thou hast none,
In death to rob me of my fame, my honour,
With such a forged lie. Tell me, thou hangman,
Where did I ever see thy face? or when
Murder'd thy sire or brothers? look on me,
And make it good: thou dar'st not.

UBERTI
Yes, I will

[He binds his arms.

In one short whisper; and that told, thou art dead.
I am Uberti: take thy sword, fight bravely;
We'll live or die together.

MARTINO
We are betray'd.

[**MARTINO** is struck down, the **SOLDIERS** run off.

FARNEZE
And have I leave once more, brave prince, to ease
My head on thy true bosom?

UBERTI
I glory more
To be thy friend, than in the name of prince,
Or any higher title.

FARNEZE
My preserver!

UBERTI
The life you gave to me I but return;.
And pardon, dearest friend, the bitter language

Necessity made me use.

FARNEZE
O, sir, I am
Outdone in all; but comforted, that none
But you can wear the laurel.

UBERTI
Here's no place
Or time to argue this; let us fly hence.

FARNEZE
I follow.

[Exeunt.

MARTINO [rises]
A thousand Furies keep you company!
I was at the gate of hell, but now I feel
My wound's not mortal; I was butastonish'd;
And, coming to myself, I find I am
Reserv'd for the gallows: there's no looking on
The enraged duke, excuses will not serve;
I must do something that may get my pardon;
If not, I know the worst, a halter ends all!

[Exit.

ACT III

SCENE I. The Dutchy of Mantua. A Part of the Country Near Octavio's Cottage

Enter **OCTAVIO**, a book in his hand.

OCTAVIO
'Tis true, by proof I find it, human reason
Views with such dim eyes what is good or ill,
That if the great Disposer of our being
Should offer to our choice all worldly blessings,
We know not what to take. When I was young,
Ambition of court-preferment fired me:
And, as there were no happiness beyond it,
I labour'd for't, and got it; no man stood
In greater favour with his prince; I had
Honours and offices, wealth flow'd in to me,
And, for my service both in peace and war,

The general voice gave out I did deserve them.
But, O vain confidence in subordinate greatness:
When I was most secure it was not in
The power of fortune to remove me from
The flat I firmly stood on, in a moment
My virtues were made crimes, and popular favour,
(To new-raised men still fatal) bred suspicion
That I was dangerous: which no sooner enter'd
Gonzaga's breast, but straight my ruin follow'd.
My offices were ta'en from me, my state seized on:
And, had I not prevented it by flight,
The jealousy of the duke had been removed
With the forfeiture of my head.

HORTENSIO [within]
Or shew compassion,
Or I will force it.

OCTAVIO
Ha! is not poverty safe?
I thought proud war, that aim'd at kingdoms' ruins,
The sack of palaces and cities, scorn' d
To look on a poor cottage.

[Enter **HORTENSIO** with **ASCANIO** in his arms, **GOTHRIO** following.

GOTHRIO
What would you have?
The devil sleeps in my pocket; I have no cross
To drive him from it. Be you or thief or soldier,
Or such a beggar as will not be denied,
My scrip, my tar-box, hook, and coat, will prove
But a thin purchase; if you turn my inside outwards,
You'll find it true.

HORTENSIO
Not any food?

[Searches his scrip.

GOTHRIO
Alas! sir,
I am no glutton, but an under-shepherd;
The very picture of famine; judge by my cheeks else:
I have my pittance by ounces, and starve myself,
When I pay a pensioner, an ancient mouse,
I have, a crumb a meal.

HORTENSIO
No drop left?

[Takes his bottle.

Drunkard! hast thou swill'd up all?

GOTHRIO
How! drunkard, sir?
I am a poor man, you mistake me, sir,
Drunkard's a title for the rich, my betters;
A carling in repute: some sell their lands for't,
And roar, Wine's better than money. Our poor beverages
Of buttermilk or whey allayed with water,
Ne'er raise our thoughts so high. Drunk, I had never
The credit to be so yet.

HORTENSIO
Ascanio,
Look up, dear youth; Ascanio, did thy sweetness
Command the greedy enemy to forbear
To prey upon it, and I thank my fortune
For suffering me to live, that in some part
I might return thy courtesies, and now,
To heighten my afflictions, must I be
Enforced, no pitying angel near to help us,
Heaven deaf to my complaints too, to behold thee
Die in my arms for hunger? no means left
To lengthen life a little! I will open
A vein, and pour my blood, not yet corrupted
With any sinful act, but pure as he is,
Into his famish'd mouth.

OCTAVIO [comes forward]
Young man, forbear
Thy savage pity; I have better means
To call back flying life.

[Pours a cordial into the mouth of **ASCANIO**.

GOTHRIO
You may believe him;
It is his sucking-bottle, and confirms,
An old man's twice a child; his nurse's milk .
Was ne'er so chargeable, should you put in too
For soap and candles: though he sell his flock for't,
The baby must have this dug: he swears 'tis ill
For my complexion; but wondrous comfortable

For an old man, that would never die.

OCTAVIO
Hope well, sir;
A temperate heat begins to thaw his numbness;
The blood too by degrees takes fresh possession
On his pale cheek; his pulse beats high stand off,
Give him more air, he stirs.

[**GOTHRIO** steals the bottle.

GOTHRIO
And have I got thee,
Thou bottle of immortality! [Aside]

ASCANIO
Where am I?
What cruel hand hath forced back wretched life?
Is rest in death denied me?

GOTHRIO
O sweet liquor!

[Drinks.

Were here enough to make me drunk, I might
Write myself gentleman, and never buy
A coat of the heralds. [Aside].

OCTAVIO
How now, slave!

GOTHRIO
I was fainting,
A clownlike qualm seized on me; but I am
Recover'd, thanks to your bottle, and begin
To feel new stirrings, gallant thoughts: one draught more
Will make me a perfect signior.

OCTAVIO
A tough cudgel
Will take this gentle itch off; home to my cottage,
See all things handsome.

GOTHRIO
Good sir, let me have
The bottle along to smell to: O rare perfume!

[Exit.

HORTENSIO
Speak once more, dear Ascanio.
How he eyes you,
Then turns away his face! look up, sweet youth;
The object cannot hurt you; this good man,
Next heaven, is your preserver.

ASCANIO
Would I'had perish'd
Without relief, rather than live to break
His good old heart with sorrow. O my shame!
My shame, my never-dying shame!

OCTAVIO
I have been
Acquainted with this voice, and know the face too:
'Tis she, 'tis too apparent; O my daughter!
I mourn 'd long for thy loss, but thus to find thee,
Is more to be lamented.

HORTENSIO
How! your daughter?

OCTAVIO
My only child; I murmur'd against heaven
Because I had no more, but now I find
This one too many. Ts Alonzo glutted

[**MARIA** weeps.

With thy embraces?

HORTENSIO
At his name, a shower
Of tears falls from her eyes; she faints again.
Grave sir, o'er-rule your passion, and defer
The story of her fortune. On my life
She is a worthy one; her innocence
Might be abused, but mischief's self wants power
To make her guilty. Shew yourself a father
In her recovery; then as a judge,
When she hath strength to speak in her own cause,
You may determine of her.

OCTAVIO
I much thank you

For your wise counsel: you direct me, sir,
As one indebted more to years, and I,
As a pupil, will obey you: not far hence
I have a homely dwelling; if you please there
To make some short repose, your entertainment,
Though coarse, shall relish of a gratitude,
And that's all I can pay you. Look up, girl,
Thou art in thy father's arms.

HORTENSIO
She's' weak and faint still spare your age!
I am young and strong, and this way
To serve her is a pleasure, not a burthen:

[Takes her in his arms.

Pray you, lead the way.

OCTAVIO
The saints reward your goodness!

[Exeunt.

SCENE II. The Same. Another Part of the Country

Enter **MANFROY**, and **MATILDA** disguised.

MATILDA
No hope of safety left?

MANFROY
We are descried.

MATILDA
I thought that, cover'd in this poor disguise,
I might have pass'd unknown.

MANFROY
A diamond,
Though set in horn, is still a diamond,
And sparkles as in purest gold. We are follow'd:
Out of the troops that scour'd the plains, I saw
Two gallant horsemen break forth, (who, by their
Brave furniture and habiliments for the war,
Seem'd to command the rest,) spurring hard towards us.
See with what winged speed they climb the hill,

Like falcons on the stretch to seize the prey!
Now they dismount, and on their hands and knees
O'ercome the deep ascent that guards us from them.
Your beauty hath betray'd you; for it can
No more be night when bright Apollo shines
In our meridian, than that be conceal'd.

MATILDA
It is my curse, not blessing; fatal to
My country, father, and myself. Why did you
Forsake the city?

MANFROY
'Twas the duke's command:
No time to argue that; we must descend.
If undiscover'd your soft feet, unused
To such rough travel, can but carry you
Half a league hence, I know a cave which will
Yield us protection.

MATILDA
I wish I could lend you
Part of my speed; for me, I can outstrip
Daphne or Atalanta.

MANFROY
Some good angel
Defend us, and strike blind our hot pursuers!

[Exeunt.

[Enter **ALONZO** and **PISANO**.

ALONSO
She cannot be far off: how gloriously
She shew'd to us in the valley!

PISANO
In my thought,
Like to a blazing comet.

ALONSO
Brighter far:
Her beams of beauty made the hill all fire;
From whence removed, 'tis cover'd with thick clouds.
But we lose time; I'll take that way.

PISANO

I, this.

[Exeunt severally.

SCENE III. The Same. A Wood

Enter **HORTENSIO**.

HORTENSIO
'Tis a degree of comfort in my sorrow,
I have done one good work in reconciling
Maria, long hid in Ascanio's habit,
To griev'd Octavio. What a sympathy
I found in their affections! she with tears
Making a free confession of her weakness,
In yielding up her honour to Alonzo,
Upon his vows to marry her; Octavio,
Prepared to credit her excuses, nay,
To extenuate her guilt; she the delinquent,
And judge, as 'twere, agreeing. But to me,
The most forlorn of men, no beam of comfort
Deigns to appear; nor can I, in my fancy,
Fashion a means to get it: to my country
I am lost for ever, and 'twere impudence
To think of a return; yet this I could
Endure with patience, but to be divorced
From all my joy on earth, the happiness
To look upon the excellence of nature,
That is perfection in herself, and needs not
Addition or epithet, rare Matilda,
Would make a saint blaspheme. Here,
Galeazzo,
In this obscure abode, 'tis fit thou shouldst
Consume thy youth, and grow old in lamenting
Thy star-cross'd fortune, in this shepherd's habit;
This hook thy best defence, since thou couldst use,
When thou didst fight in such a princess' cause,
Thy sword no better.

[Lies down.

[Enter **ALONZO** and **PISANO** with **MATILDA**.

MATILDA
Are you men, or monsters?
Whither will you drag me? can the open ear

Of heaven be deaf, when an unspotted maid
Cries out for succour!

PISANO
'Tis in vain; cast lots
Who shall enjoy her first.

ALONSO
Flames rage within me,
And, such a spring of nectar near to quench them!
My appetite shall be cloy 'd first: here I stand,
Thy friend, or enemy; let me have precedence,
I write a friend's name in my heart; deny it,
As an enemy I defy thee.

PISANO
Friend or foe
In this alike I value, I disdain
To yield priority; draw thy sword.

ALONSO
To sheath it
In thy ambitious heart.

MATILDA
O curb this fury,
And hear a wretched maid first speak.

HORTENSIO
I am marble.

MATILDA
Where shall I seek out words, or how restrain
My enemies rage, or lovers'? oh, the latter
Is far more odious: did not your lust
Provoke you, for that is its proper name,
My chastity were safe; and yet I tremble more
To think what dire effects lust may bring, forth,
Than what, as enemies, you can inflict,
And less I fear it. Be friends to yourselves,
And enemies to me; better I fall
A sacrifice to your atonement, than
Or one or both should perish. I am the cause
Of your division; remove it, lords,
And concord will spring up: poison this face
That hath bewitch'd you, this grove cannot want
Aspics or toads; creatures, though justly call'd,
For their deformity, the scorn of nature,

More happy than myself with this false beauty
(The seed and fruit of mischief) you admire so.
I thus embrace your knees, and yours, a suppliant,
If tigers did not nurse you, or you suck
The milk of a fierce lioness, shew compassion
Unto yourselves in being reconciled,
And pity to poor me, my honour safe,
In taking loath'd life from me.

PISANO
What shall we do?
Or end our difference in killing her,
Or fight it out?

ALONSO
To the last gasp. I feel
The moist tears on my cheeks, and blush to find
A virgin's plaints can move so.

PISANO
To prevent
Her flight while we contend, let's bind her fast
To this cypress-tree.

ALONSO
Agreed.

MATILDA
It does presage
My funeral rites.

[They bind **MATILDA**.

HORTENSIO
I shall turn atheist
If heaven see and suffer this: why did I
Abandon my good sword? with unarm 'd hands
I cannot rescue her. Some angel pluck me
From the apostacy I am falling to.
And by a miracle lend me a weapon
To underprop falling honour.

PISANO
She is fast:
Resume your arms.

ALONSO
Honour, revenge, the maid too,

Lie at the stake.

PISANO
Which thus I draw.

[They fight, **PISANO** falls.

ALONSO
All's mine,
But bought with some blood of mine own.
Pisano,
Thou wert a noble enemy, wear that laurel
In death to comfort thee: for the reward,
Tis mine now without rival.

[**HORTENSIO** snatches up Pisano's sword.

HORTENSIO
Thou art deceived;
Men will grow up like to the dragon's teeth
From Cadmus' helm, sown in the field of Mars,
To guard pure chastity from lust and rape.
Libidinous monster, satyr, faun, or what
Does better speak thee, slave to appetite,
And sensual baseness; if thy profane hand
But touch this virgin temple, thou art dead.

MATILDA
I see the aid of heaven, though slow, is sure.

ALONSO
A rustic swain dare to retard my pleasure!

HORTENSIO
No swain, Alonzo, but her knight and servant
To whom the world should owe and pay obedience;
One that thou hast encounter'd, and shrunk under
His arm; that spared thy life in the late battle,
At the intercession of the princess' page.
Look on me better.

MATILDA
'Tis my virtuous lover!
Under his guard 'twere sin to doubt my safety.

ALONSO
I know thee, and with courage will redeem
What fortune then took from me.

HORTENSIO
Rather keep

[They fight, **ALONZO** falls.

Thy compeer company in death. Lie by him,
A prey for crows and vultures: these fair arms,

[He unbinds **MATILDA**.

Unfit for bonds, should have been chains to make
A bridegroom happy, though a prince, and proud
Of such captivity: whatsoe'er you are,
I glory in the service I have done you;
But I entreat you pay your vows and prayers,
For preservation of your life and honour,
To the most virtuous princess, chaste Matilda.
I am her creature, and what good I do
'You truly may call hers; what's ill, mine own.

MATILDA
You never did do ill, my virtuous servant;
Nor is it in the power of poor Matilda,
To cancel such an obligation as,
With humble willingness, she must subscribe to.

HORTENSIO
The princess? ha!

MATILDA
Give me a fitter name,
Your manumised bondwoman, but even now
In the possession of lust, from which
Your more than brave, heroic valour bought me:
And can I then, for freedom unexpected,
But kneel to you, my patron?

HORTENSIO
Kneel to me!
For heaven's sake rise; I kiss the ground you tread on,
My eyes fix'd on the earth; for I confess
I am a thing not worthy to look on you,
Till you have sign'd my pardon.

MATILDA
Do you interpret
The much good you have done me, an offence?

HORTENSIO

The not performing your injunctions to me,
Is more than capital: your allowance of
My love and service to you, with admission
To each place you made paradise with your presence,
Should have enabled me to bring home conquest;
Then, as a sacrifice, to offer it
At the altar of your favour: had my love
Answer'd your bounty, or my hopes, an army
Had been as dust before me; whereas I,
Like a coward, turn'd my back, and durst not stand
The fury of the enemy.

MATILDA

Had you done
Nothing in the battle, this last act deserves more
Than I, the duke my father joining with me,
Can ever recompense. But take your pleasure;
Suppose you have offended in not grasping
Your boundless hopes, I thus seal on your lips
A full remission.

HORTENSIO

Let mine touch your foot,
Your hand's too high a favour.

MATILDA

Will you force me
To ravish a kiss from you?

[Kisses him.

HORTENSIO

I am entranced.

MATILDA

So much desert and bashfulness should not march
In the same file. Take comfort; when you have brought me
To some place of security, you shall find
You have a seat here, in a heart that hath
Already studied and vow'd to be thankful.

HORTENSIO

Heaven make me so! oh, I am overwhelm 'd
With an excess of joy! Be not too prodigal,
Divinest lady, of your grace and bounties,
At once; if you are pleased, I shall enjoy them,

Not taste them, and expire.

MATILDA
I'll be more sparing.

[Exeunt.

[Enter **OCTAVIO**, **GOTHRIO**, and **MARIA**.

OCTAVIO
What noise of clashing swords, like armour fashion'd
Upon an anvil, pierced mine ears; the echo
Redoubling the loud sound through all the vallies?
This way the wind assures me that it came.

GOTHRIO
Then with your pardon, I'll take this.

OCTAVIO
Why, sirrah?

GOTHRIO
Because, sir, I will trust my heels before
All winds that blow in the sky: we are wiser far
Than our grandsires were, and in this I'll prove it;
They said, Haste to the beginning of a feast,
There I am with them; but to the end of a fray
That is apocryphal; 'tis more canonical,
Not to come there at all; after a storm
There are still some drops behind.

MARIA
Pure fear hath made
The fool a philosopher.

OCTAVIO
See, Maria, see!
I did not err; here lie two brave men weltering
In their own gore.

MARIA
A pitiful object.

GOTHRIO
I am in a swoon to look on't.

OCTAVIO
They are stiff already.

GOTHRIO
But are you sure they are dead?

OCTAVIO
Too sure, I fear.

GOTHRIO
But are they stark dead?

OCTAVIO
Leave prating.

GOTHRIO
Then I am valiant, and dare come nearer to them.
This fellow without a sword shall be my patient.

[Goes to **PISANO**.

OCTAVIO
Whate'er they are, humanity commands us
To do our best endeavour. Run, Maria,
To the neighbour spring for water; you will find there
A wooden dish, the beggar's plate, to bring it.

[Exit **MARIA**.

Why dost not, dull drone, bend his body, and feel
If any life remain?

GOTHRIO
By your leave, he shall die first,
And then I'll be his surgeon.

OCTAVIO
Tear ope his doublet,
And prove if his wounds be mortal.

GOTHRIO
Fear not me, sir:
Here's a large wound.

[Feels his pocket.

How it is swoln and imposthumed!
This must be cunningly drawn out; should it break,

[Pulls out his purse.

'Twould strangle him. What a deal of foul matter's here!
This hath been long a gathering. Here's a gash too
On the rim of his belly, it may have matter in it.

[Feels his side pocket.

He was a choleric man, sure; what comes from him

[Takes out his money.

Is yellow as gold: how! troubled with the stone too?

[Seeing a diamond ring on his finger.

I'll cut you for this.

PISANO
Oh, oh!

[Starts up.

GOTHRIO
He roars before I touch him.

PISANO
Robb'd of my life?

GOTHRIO
No, sir, nor of your money,
Nor jewel; I keep them for you: if I had been
A perfect mountebank, he had not lived
To call for his fees again.

OCTAVIO
Give me leave there's hope
Of his recovery.

[Quits **PISANO** and goes to **ALONZO**.

GOTHRIO
I had rather bury him quick,
Than part with my purchase; let his ghost walk, I care not.

[Re-enter **MARIA** with a dish of water.

OCTAVIO
Well done, Maria; lend thy helping hand.

He hath a deep wound in his head, wash off
The clotted blood: he comes to himself.

ALONSO
My lust!
The fruit that grows upon the tree of lust
With horror now I taste it.

OCTAVIO
Do you not know him?

MARIA
Too soon. Alonzo! oh me! though disloyal,
Still dear to thy Maria.

GOTHRIO
So they know not
My patient, all's cocksure; I do not like
The Romanish restitution [Aside]

OCTAVIO
Rise, and leave him.
Applaud heaven's justice.

MARIA
'Twill become me better,
To implore its saving mercy.

OCTAVIO
Hast thou no gall?
No feeling of thy wrongs?

MARIA
Turtles have none;
Nor can there be such poison in her breast
That truly loves, and lawfully.

OCTAVIO
True, if that love
Be placed on a worthy subject. What he is.
In thy disgrace is published; heaven hath mark'd him
For punishment, and 'twere rebellious madness
In thee to attempt to alter it: revenge,
A sovereign balm for injuries, is more proper
To thy robb'd honour. Join with me, and thou
Shalt be thyself the goddess of revenge,
This wretch, the vassal of thy wrath: I'll make him,
While yet he lives, partake those torments which,

For perjured lovers, are prepared in hell,
Before his curs'd ghost enter it. This oil,
Extracted and sublimed from all the simples
The earth, when swoln with venom, e'er brought forth,
Pour'd in his wounds, shall force such anguish as
The Furies whips but imitate; and when
Extremity of pain shall hasten death.
Here is another that shall keep in life,
And make him feel a perpetuity
Of lingering tortures.

GOTHRIO
Knock them both o" th' head, I say,
An it be but for their skins; they are embroider'd,
And will sell well in the market.

MARIA
Ill-look'd devil,
Tie up thy bloody tongue. O sir! I was slow
In beating down those propositions which
You urge for my revenge; my reasons being
So many, and so forcible, that make
Against yours, that until I had collected
My scattered powers, I waver 'd in my choice
Which I should first deliver. Fate hath brought
My enemy (I can faintly call him so)
Prostrate before my feet; shall I abuse
Tke bounty of my fate, by trampling on him?
He alone ruin'd me, nor can any hand
But his rebuild my late demolish'd honour.
If you deny me means of reparation,
To satisfy your spleen, you are more cruel
Than ever yet Alonzo was; you stamp
The name of strumpet on my forehead, which
Heaven's mercy would take off; you fan the fire,
E'en ready to go out; forgetting that
'Tis truly noble, having power to punish,
Nay, kinglike, to forbear it. I would purchase
My husband by such benefits as should make him
Confess himself my equal, and disclaim
Superiority.

OCTAVIO
My blessing on thue!
What I urged was a trial; and my grant
To thy desires shall now appear, if art
Or long experience can do him sen-ice.
Nor shall my charity to this be wanting,

Howe'er unknown: help me, Maria: you, sir,
Do your best to raise him. So!

GOTHRIO
He's wondrous heavy;
But the porter's paid, there's the comfort.

OCTAVIO
Tis but a trance,
And 'twill forsake both.

MARIA
If he live, I fear not
He will redeem all, and in thankfulness
Confirm he owes you for a second life,
And pay the debt, in making me his wife.

[Exeunt **OCTAVIO** and **MARIA** with **ALONZO**, and **GOTHRIO** with **PISANO**.

ACT IV

SCENE I. Lorenzo's Camp Under the Walls of Mantua

Enter **LORENZO** and **CAPTAINS**.

LORENZO
Mantua is ours; place a strong garrison in it,
To keep it so; and as a due reward
To your brave service, be our governour in it.

1ST CAPTAIN
I humbly thank your excellence.

[Exit.

LORENZO
Gonzaga
Is yet out of our gripe; but his strong fort,
St. Leo, which he holds impregnable
By the aids of art, as nature, shall not long
Retard our absolute conquest. The escape
Of fair Matilda, my supposed mistress,
(For whose desired possession 'twas given out
I made this war,) I value not j alas!
Cupid's too feeble-eyed to hit my heart,
Or could he see, his arrows are too blunt

To pierce it; his imagined torch is quench 'd
With a more glorious fire of my ambition
To enlarge my empire: soft and silken amours,
With carpet courtship, which weak princes style
The happy issue of a flourishing peace,
My toughness scorns. Were there an abstract made
Of all the eminent and canonized beauties
By truth recorded, or by poets feign'd,
I could unmoved behold it; as a picture,
Commend the workmanship, and think no more on't;
I have more noble ends. Have you not heard yet
Of Alonzo, or Pisano?

2ND CAPTAIN
My lord, of neither.

LORENZO
Two turbulent spirits unfit for discipline,
Much less command in war; if they were lost,
I should not pine with mourning.

[Enter **MARTINO** and **SOLDIERS** with **MATILDA** and **HORTENSIO**.

MARTINO
Bring them forward:
This will make my peace, though I had kill'd his father;
Besides the reward that follows.

LORENZO
Ha, Martino!
Where is Farneze's head? dost thou stare! and where
The soldier that desired the torture of him?

MARTINO
An't please your excellence

LORENZO
It doth not please us;
Are our commands obey'd?

MARTINO
Farneze's head, sir,
Is a thing not worth your thought, the soldier's less, sir:
I have brought your highness such a head! a head
So well set on too! a fine head

LORENZO
Take that,

[Strikes him.

For thy impertinence: what head, you rascal?

MARTINO
My lord, if they that bring such presents to you
Are thus rewarded, there are few will strive
To be near your grace's pleasures: but I know
You will repent your choler. Here's the head:
And now I draw the curtain, it hath a face too,
And such a face

LORENZO
Ha!

MARTINO
View her all o'er, my lord,
My company on't, she's sound of wind and limb,
And will do her labour tightly, a bona roba:
And for her face, as I said, there are five hundred
City-dubb'd madams in the dukedom, that would part with
Their jointures to have such another: hold up your head, maid.

LORENZO
Of what age is the day?

MARTINO
Sir, since sunrising
About two hours.

LORENZO
Thou liest; the sun of beauty,
In modest blushes on her cheeks, but now
Appear'd to me, and in her tears breaks forth,
As through a shower in April; every drop
An orient pearl, which, as it falls, congeal'd,
Were ear-rings for the Catholic king, to be
Worn on his birthday.

MARTINO
Here's a sudden change!

LORENZO
Incensed Cupid, whom even now I scorn'd,
Hath ta'en his stand, and by reflection shines
(As if he had two bodies, or indeed
A brother-twin whom sight cannot distinguish)

In her fair eyes: see, how they head their arrows
With her bright beams! now frown, as if my heart,
Rebellious to their edicts, were unworthy,
Should I rip up my bosom, to receive
A wound from such divine artillery!

MARTINO [Aside]
I am made for ever.

MATILDA
We are lost, dear servant.

HORTENSIO
Virtue's but a word;
Fortune rules all.

MATILDA
We are her tennis-balls.

LORENZO
Allow her fair, her symmetry and features
So well proportion'd, as the heavenly object
With admiration would strike Ovid dumb,
Nay, force him to forget his faculty
In verse, and celebrate her praise in prose.
What's this to me? I that have pass'd my youth
Unscorch'd with wanton fires, my sole delight:
In glittering arms, my conquering sword my mistress,
Neighing of barbed horse, the cries and groans
Of vanquish'd foes suing for life, my music:
And shall I, in the autumn of my age,
Now, when I wear the livery of time
Upon my head and beard, suffer myself
To be transform'd, and like a puling lover,
With arms thus folded up, echo Ah me'sf
And write myself a bondman to my vassal?
It must not, nay, it shall not be: remove
The object, and the effect dies. Nearer,
Martino.

MARTINO
I shall have a regiment: colonel Martino,
I cannot go less.

LORENZO
What thing is this thou hast brought me?

MARTINO

What thing? heaven bless me! are you a Florentine,
Nay, the great duke of Florentines, and having had her
So long in your power, do you now ask what she is?
Take her aside and learn: I have brought you that
I look to be dearly paid for.

LORENZO
I am a soldier,
And use of women will, Martino, rob
My nerves of strength.

MARTINO
All armour and no smock?
Abominable! a little of the one with the other
Is excellent: I ne'er knew general yet,
Nor prince that did deserve to be a worthy,
But he desired to have his sweat wash'd off
By a juicy bedfellow.

LORENZO
But say she be unwilling
To do that office?

MARTINO
Wrestle with her, I will wager
Ten to one on your grace's side.

LORENZO
Slave, hast thou brought me
Temptation in a beauty not to be
With prayers resisted; and, in place of counsel
To master my affections, and to guard
My honour, now besieged by lust, with the arms
Of sober temperance, mark me out a way
To be a ravisher? Would thou hadst shewn me
Some monster, though in a more ugly form
Than Nile or Afric ever bred! The basilisk,
Whose envious eye yet never brook'd a neighbour,
Kills but the body; her more potent eye
Buries alive mine honour: Shall I yield thus?
And all brave thoughts of victory and triumphs,
The spoils of nations, the loud applauses
Of happy subjects, made so by my conquests;
And, what's the crown of all, a glorious name
Insculp'd on pyramids to posterity,
Be drench'd in Lethe, and no object take me
But a weak woman, rich in colours only,
Too delicate a touch, and some rare features

Which age or sudden sickness will take from her!
And where's then the reward of all my service,
Love-soothing passions, nay, idolatry
I must pay to her? Hence, and with thee take
This second but more dangerous Pandora,
Whose fatal box, if open'd, will pour on me
All mischiefs that mankind is subject to.
To the desarts with this Circe, this Calypso,
This fair enchantress! let her spells and charms
Work upon beasts and thee, than whom wise nature
Ne'er made a viler creature.

MATILDA
Happy exile!

HORTENSIO
Some spark of hope remains yet.

MARTINO
Come, you are mine now.
I will remove her where your highness shall not
Or see or hear more of her: what a sum
Will she yield for the Turk's seraglio!

LORENZO
Stay, I feel
A sudden alteration.

MARTINO
Here are fine whimsies.

LORENZO
Why should I part with her? can any foulness
Inhabit such a clean and gorgeous palace?
The fish, the fowl, the beasts, may safer leave
The elements they were nourish'd in, and live,
Than I endure her absence; yet her presence
Is a torment to me: why do I call it so?
My sire enjoy'd a woman, I had not been else;
He was a complete prince, and shall I blush
To follow his example? Oh! but my choice,
Though she gave suffrage to it, is beneath me:
But even now, in my proud thoughts, I scorn'd
A princess, fair Matilda; and is't decreed
For punishment, I straight must dote on one,
What, or from whence, I know not? Grant she be
Obscure, without a coat or family,
Those I can give: and yet, if she were noble,

My fondness were more pardonable. Martino,
Dost thou know thy prisoner?

MARTINO
Do I know myself?
I kept that for the 1'envoy; 'tis the daughter
Of your enemy, duke Gonzaga.

LORENZO
Fair Matilda!
I now call to my memory her picture,
And find this is the substance; but her painter
Did her much wrong, I see it.

MARTINO
I am sure
I tugg'd hard for her, here are wounds can witness,
Before I could call her mine.

LORENZO
No matter how:
Make thine own ransome, I will pay it for her.

MARTINO
I knew 'twould come at last.

MATILDA
We are lost again.

HORTENSIO
Variety of afflictions!

LORENZO
That his knee,
That never yet bow'd to mortality,

[Kneels.

Kisses the earth happy to bear your weight,
I know , begets your wonder; hear the reason,.
And cast it off: your beauty does command it.
Till now, I never saw you; fame hath been
Too sparing in report of your perfections,
Which now with admiration I gaze on.
Be not afraid, fair virgin; had you been
Employ 'd to mediate your father's cause,
My drum had been unbraced, my trumpet hung up;
Nor had the terror of the war e'er frighted

His peaceful confines; your demands had been,
As soon as spoke, agreed to: but you'll answer,
And may w'th reason, words make no satisfaction
For what's in fact committed. Yet, take comfort,
Something my pious love commands me do,
Which may call down your pardon.

MATILDA
This expression
Of reverence to your person better suits

[Raises **LORENZO**, and kneels.

With my low fortune. That you deign to love me,
My weakness would persuade me to believe,
Though conscious of mine own unworthiness
You being as the liberal eye of heaven,
Which may shine where it pleases, let your beams
Of favour warm and comfort, not consume me!
For, should your love grow to excess, I dare not
Deliver what I fear.

LORENZO
Dry your fair eyes;
I apprehend your doubts, and could be angry,
If humble love could warrant it, you should
Nourish such base thoughts of me. Heaven bear witness,
And, if I break my vow, dart thunder at me,
You are, and shall be, in my tent as free
From fear of violence, as a cloister'd nun
Kneeling before the altar. What I purpose
Is yet an embryo; but, grown into form,
I'll give you power to be the sweet disposer
Of blessings unexpected; that your father,
Your country, people, children yet unborn too,
In holy hymns, on festivals, shall sing
The triumph of your beauty. On your hand
Once more I swear it: O imperious Love,
Look down, and, as I truly do repent,
Prosper the good ends of thy penitent!

[Exeunt.

SCENE II. The Dutchy. A Room in Octavio's Cottage

Enter **OCTAVIO**, disguised as a Priest, and **MARIA**.

OCTAVIO
You must not be too sudden, my Maria,
In being known: I am, in this friar's habit,
As yet conceal'd. Though his recovery
Be almost certain, I must work him to
Repentance by degrees; when I would have you
Appear in your true shape of sorrow, to
Move his compassion, I will stamp thus, then,
You know to act your part.

MARIA
I shall be careful.

[Exit.

OCTAVIO
If I can cure the ulcers of his mind,
As I despair not of his body's wounds,
Felicity crowns my labour. Gothrio!

[Enter **GOTHRIO**.

GOTHRIO
Here, sir.

OCTAVIO
Desire my patients to leave their chamber,
And take fresh air here: how have they slept

GOTHRIO
Very well, sir.
I would we were so rid of them.

OCTAVIO
Why?

GOTHRIO
I fear one hath
The art of memory, and will remember
His gold and jewels: could you not minister
A potion of forgetfulness? What would gallants
That are in debt give me for such a receipt,
To pour in their creditors' drink?

OCTAVIO
You shall restore all,
Believe 't, you shall: will you please to walk?

GOTHRIO
Will you please to put off
Your holy habit, and spiced conscience? one,
I think, infects the other.

[Exit.

OCTAVIO
I have observed
Compunction in Alonzo; he speaks little,
But full of retired thoughts: the other is
Jocund and merry; no doubt, because he hath
The less accompt to make here.

[Enter **ALONZO**.

ALONSO
Reverend sir,
I come to wait your pleasure; but, my friend,
Your creature I should say, being so myself,
Willing to take further repose, entreats
Your patience a few minutes.

OCTAVIO
At his pleasure;
Pray you sit down; you are faint still.

ALONSO
Growing to strength,
I thank your goodness: but my mind is troubled,
Very much troubled, sir, and I desire,
Your pious habit giving me assurance
Of your skill and power that way, that you would please
To be my mind's physician.

OCTAVIO
Sir, to that
My order binds me; if you please to unload
The burthen of your conscience, I will minister
Such heavenly cordials as I can, and set you
In a path that leads to comfort.

ALONSO
I will open
My bosom's secrets to you. That I am
A man of blood, being brought up in the wars,
And cruel executions, my profession

Admits not to be question'd; but in that,
Being a subject, and bound to obey
Whate'er my prince commanded, I have left
Some shadow of excuse: with other crimes,
As pride, lust, gluttony, it must be told,
I am besmear'd all over.

OCTAVIO
On repentance,
Mercy will wash it off.

ALONSO
O sir, I grant
These sins are deadly ones; yet their frequency
With wicked men makes them less dreadful to us.
But I am conscious of one crime, with which
All ills I have committed from my youth
Put in the scale, weigh nothing; such a crime,
So odious to heaven and man, and to
My sear'd-up conscience so full of horror,
As penance cannot expiate.

OCTAVIO
Despair not.
Tis impious in man to prescribe limits
To the divine compassion: out with it.

ALONSO
Hear then, good man, and when that I have given you
The character of it, and confess'd myself
The wretch that acted it, you must repent
The charity you have extended towards me.
Not long before these wars began, I had
Acquaintance ('tis not fit I style it friendship,
That being a virtue, and not to be blended
With vicious breach of faith) with the lord
Octavio,
The minion of his prince and court, set off
With all the pomp and circumstance of greatness:
To this then happy man I offer'd service,
And with insinuation wrought myself
Into his knowledge, grew familiar with him,
Ever a welcome guest. This noble gentleman
Was bless'd with one fair daughter, so he thought,
And boldly might believe so, for she was
In all things excellent without a rival,
Till I, her father's mass of wealth before
My greedy eyes, but hoodwink'd to mine honour,

With far more subtile arts than perjured Paris
E'er practised on poor credulous Œnone,
Besieged her virgin fort, in a word, took it,
No vows or imprecation forgotten
With speed to marry her.

OCTAVIO
Perhaps, she gave you
Just cause to break those vows.

ALONZO
She cause! alas,
Her innocence knew no guilt, but too much favour
To me, unworthy of it: 'twas my baseness,
My foul ingratitude what shall I say more?
The good Octavio no sooner fell
In the displeasure of his prince, his state
Confiscated, and he forced to leave the court,
And she exposed to want; but all my oaths
And protestation of service to her,
Like seeming flames raised by enchantment, vanish'd;
This, this sits heavy here.

OCTAVIO
He speaks as if
He were acquainted with my plot. You have reason
To feel compunction, for 'twas most inhuman
So to betray a maid.

ALONSO
Most barbarous.

OCTAVIO
But does your sorrow for the fact beget
An aptness in you to make satisfaction
For the wrong you did her?

ALONSO
Gracious heaven! an aptness?
It is my only study: since I tasted
Of your compassion, these eyes ne'er were closed,
But fearful dreams cut off my little sleep;
And, being awake, in my imagination
Her apparition haunted me.

OCTAVIO
'Twas mere fancy.

[He stamps.

ALONSO
'Twas more, grave sir nay, 'tis now it appears!

[Enter **MARIA**, in white.

OCTAVIO
Where?

ALONSO
Do you not see there the gliding shadow
Of a fair virgin? that is she, and wears
The very garments that adorn'd her, when
She yielded to my crocodile tears: a cloud
Of fears and diffidence then so chased away
Her purer white and red, as it foretold
That I should be disloyal. Blessed shadow!
For 'twere a sin, far, far exceeding all
I have committed, to hope only that
Thou art a substance; look on my true sorrow,
Nay, soul's contrition: hear again those vows
My perjury cancell'd, stamp'd in brass, and never
To be worn out.

MARIA
I can endure no more;
Action, not oaths, must make me reparation:
I am Maria.

ALONSO
Can this be?

OCTAVIO
It is,
And I Octavio.

ALONSO
Wonder on wonder!
How shall I look on you, or with what forehead
Desire your pardon?

MARIA
You truly shall deserve it
In being constant.

[Re-enter **GOTHRIO**, with the purses of **ALONZO** and **PISANO**.

OCTAVIO
If you fall not off,
But look on her in poverty with those eyes
As, when she was my heir in expectation,
You thought her beautiful.

ALONSO
She is in herself
Both Indies to me.

GOTHRIO
Stay, she shall not come
A beggar to you, my sweet young mistress no,
She shall not want a dower: here's white and red
Will ask a jointure; but how you should make her one,
Being a captain, would beget some doubt,
If you should deal with a lawyer.

ALONSO
I have seen this purse.

GOTHRIO
How the world's given I dare not say, to lying,
Because you are a soldier; you may say as well,
This gold is mark'd too: you, being to receive it,
Should ne'er ask how I got it. I'll run for a priest
To dispatch the matter; you shall not want a ring,
I have one for the purpose.

[Gives Pisano's ring to **ALONZO**.

Now, sir, I think I'm honest.

[Exit.

ALONSO
This ring was Pisano's.

OCTAVIO
I'll dissolve this riddle
At better leisure: the wound given to my daughter,
Which, in your honour, you are bound to cure,
Exacts our present care.

ALONSO
I am all yours, sir.

[Exeunt.

Enter **GONZAGA**, **UBERTI**, and **MANFROY**.

GONZAGA
Thou hast told too much to give assurance that
Her honour was too far engaged, to be
By human help redeem 'd: if thou hadst given
Thy sad narration this full period,
She's dead, I had been happy.

UBERTI
Sir, these tears
Do well become a father, and my eyes
Would keep you company as a forlorn lover,
But that the burning fire of my revenge
Dries up those drops of sorrow. We once more,
Our broken forces rallied up, and with
Full numbers strengthen'd, stand prepared t' endure
A second trial; nor let it dismay us
That we are once again to affront the fury
Of a victorious army; their abuse
Of conquest hath disarm 'd them, and call'd down
The Powers above to aid us. I have read
Some piece of story, yet ne'er found but that.
The general, that gave way to cruelty,
The profanation of things sacred, rapes
Of virgins, butchery of infants, and
The massacre in cold blood of reverend age,
Against the discipline and law of arms,
Did feel the hand of heaven lie heavy on him,
When most secure. We have had a late example,
And let us not despair but that, in Lorenzo,
It will be seconded.

GONZAGA
You argue well,
And 'twere a sin in me to contradict you:
Yet we must not neglect the means that's lent us,
To be the ministers of justice.

UBERTI
No, sir:
One day given to refresh our wearied troops,
Tired with a tedious march, we'll be no longer

Coop'd up, but charge the enemy in his trenches,
And force him to a battle.

[Shouts within.

GONZAGA
Ha! how's this?

In such a general time of mourning, shouts,.
And acclamations of joy?

[Cry within, Long live the princess! long live Matilda!

UBERTI
Matilda!
The princess' name, Matilda, oft re-echoed!

[Enter **FARNEZE**.

GONZAGA
What speaks thy haste?

FARNEZE
More joy and happiness
Than weak words can deliver, or strong faith
Almost give credit to: the princess lives;
I saw her, kiss'd her hand.

GONZAGA
By whom deliver'd?

FARNEZE
This is not to be staled by my report,
This only must be told: As I rode forth
With some choice troops, to make discovery
Where the enemy lay, and how intrench'd, a leader
Of the adverse party, but unarm'd, and in
His hand an olive branch, encounter'd me:
He shew'd the great duke's seal, that gave him power
To parley with me; his desires were, that
Assurance for his safety might be granted
To his royal master, who came as a friend,
And not as an enemy, to offer to you
Conditions of peace. I yielded to it.
This being return'd, the duke's prostorium open'd,
When suddenly, in a triumphant chariot
Drawn by such soldiers of his own as were,
For insolence after victory, condemn'd

Unto this slavish office, the fair princess
Appear'd, a wreath of laurel on her head,
Her robes majestical, their richness far
Above all value, as the present age
Contended that a woman's pomp should dim
The glittering triumphs of the Roman
Caesars.

[Music without.

I am cut off; no cannon's throat now thunders,
Nor fife nor drum beat up a charge; choice music
Ushers the parent of security,
Long-absent peace.

MANFROY
I know not what to think on't.

UBERTI
May it poise the expectation!

[Loud music. Enter **SOLDIERS** unarmed, tearing olive branches, **CAPTAINS**, **LORENZO**, **MATILDA** crowned with a wreath of laurel, and seated in a chariot drawn by **SOLDIERS**; followed by **HORTENSIO** and **MARTINO**.

GONZAGA
Thus to meet you,
Great duke of Tuscany, throws amazement on me;
But to behold my daughter, long since mourn'd for,
And lost even to my hopes, thus honour'd by you,
With an excess of comfort overwhelms me:
And yet I cannot truly call myself
Happy in this solemnity, till your highness
Vouchsafe to make me understand the motive
That, in this peaceful way, hath brought you to us.

LORENZO
I must crave license first; for know,
Gonzaga,
I am subject to another's will, and can
Nor speak nor do without permission from her,
My curled forehead, of late terrible
To those that did acknowledge me their lord,
Is now as smooth as rivers when no wind stirs;
My frowns or smiles, that kill'd or saved, have lost
Their potent awe, and sweetness: I am transform'd
(But do not scorn the metamorphosis)
From that fierce thing men held me; I am captived,

And, by the unresistible force of beauty,
Led hither as a prisoner. Is't your pleasure that
I shall deliver those injunctions which
Your absolute command imposed upon me,
Or deign yourself to speak them?

MATILDA
Sir, I am
Your property, you may use me as you please;
But what is in your power and breast to do,
No orator can dilate so well.

LORENZO
I obey you.
That I came hither as an enemy,
With hostile arms, to the utter ruin of
Your country, what I have done makes apparent;
That fortune seconded my will, the late
Defeature will make good: that I resolved
To force the sceptre from your hand, and make
Your dukedom tributary, my surprisal
Of Mantua, your metropolis, can well witness;
And that I cannot fear the change of fate,
My army flesh'd in blood, spoil, glory, conquest,
Stand ready to maintain: yet, I must tell you
By whom I am subdued, and what's the ransome
| I am commanded to lay down.

GONZAGA
My lord,
You humble yourself too much; it is fitter
You should propose, and we consent.

LORENZO
Forbear,
The articles are here subscribed and sign'd
By my obedient hand: all prisoners,
Without a ransome, set at liberty;
Mantua to be deliver'd up, the rampires
Ruin'd in the assault, to be repair'd;
The loss the husbandman received, his crop
Burnt up by wanton license of the soldier,
To be made good; with whatsoever else
You could impose on me, if you had been
The conqueror, I your captive.

GONZAGA
Such a change

Wants an example: I must owe this favour
To the clemency of the old heroic valour,
That spared when it had power to kill; a virtue
Buried long since, but raised out of the grave
By you, to grace this latter age.

LORENZO
Mistake not
The cause that did produce this good effect,
If as such you receive it: 'twas her beauty,
Wrought first on my rough nature; but the virtues
Of her fair soul, dilated in her converse,
That did confirm it.

MATILDA
Mighty sir, no more:
You honour her too much, that is not worthy
To be your servant.

LORENZO
I have done, and now
Would gladly understand that you allow of
The articles propounded.

GONZAGA
Do not wrong
Your benefits with such a doubt; they are
So great and high, and with such reverence
To be received, that, if I should profess
I hold my dukedom from you, as your vassal,
Or offer'd up my daughter as you please
To be disposed of, in the point of honour,
And a becoming gratitude, 'twould not cancel
The bond I stand engaged for: but accept
Of that which I can pay, my all is yours, sir;
Nor is there any here, (though I must grant
Some have deserved much from me,) for so far
I dare presume, but will surrender up
Their interest to that your highness shall
Deign to pretend a title.

UBERTI
I subscribe not
To this condition.

FARNEZE
The services
This prince hath done your grace in your most danger,

Are not to be so slighted.

HORTENSIO
'Tis far from me
To urge my merits, yet, I must maintain,
Howe'er my power is less, my love is more;
Nor will the gracious princess scorn to acknowledge
I have been her humble servant.

LORENZO
Smooth your brows,
I'll not encroach upon your right, for that were
Once more to force affection, (a crime
With which should I the second time be tainted,
I did deserve no favour,) neither will I
Make use of what is ofter'd by the duke,
Howe'er I thank his goodness. I'll lay by
My power, and though I should not brook a rival,
(What we are, well consider'd,) I'll descend
To be a third competitor; he that can
With love and service best deserve the garland,
With your consent let him wear it; I despair not
The trial of my fortune.

GONZAGA
Bravely offer'd,
And like yourself, great prince.

UBERTI
I must profess
I am so taken with it, that I know not
Which way to express my service.

HORTENSIO
Did I not build
Upon the princess' grace, I could sit down,
And hold it no dishonour.

MATILDA
How I feel
My soul divided! all have deserved so well,
I know not where to fix my choice.

GONZAGA
You have
Time to consider: will you please to take
Possession of the fort? then, having tasted
The fruits of peace, you may at leisure prove,

Whose plea will prosper in the court of Love.

[Exeunt.

Enter **ALONZO, OCTAVIO, PISANO, MARIA**, and **GOTHRIO**.

ALONSO
You need not doubt, sir, were not peace proclaim'd
And celebrated with a general joy,
The high displeasure of the Mantuan duke,
Raised on just grounds, not jealous suppositions,
The saving of our lives (which, next to heaven,
To you alone is proper) would force mercy
For an offence, though capital.

PISANO
When the conqueror
Uses entreaties, they are arm'd commands
The vanquish'd must not check at.

MARIA
My piety pay the forfeit,
If danger come but near you! I have heard
My gracious mistress often mention you,
When I served her as a page, and feelingly
Relate how much the duke her sire repented
His hasty doom of banishment, in his rage
Pronounced against you.

OCTAVIO
In a private difference,
I grant that innocence is a wall of brass,
And scorns the hottest battery; but, when
The cause depends between the prince and subject,
'Tis an unequal competition; Justice
Must lay her balance by, and use her sword
For his ends that protects it. I was banish'd,
And, till revoked from exile, to tread on
My sovereign's territories with forbidden feet,
The severe letter of the law calls death;
Which I am subject to, in coming so near
His court and person. But my only child

Being provided for, her honour salved too,
I thank your noble change, I shall endure
Whate'er can fall, with patience.

ALONSO
You have used
That medicine too long; prepare yourself
For honour in your age, and rest secure oft.

MARIA
Of what is your wisdom musing?

GOTHRIO
I am gazing on
This gorgeous house; our cote's a dishclout to it;
It has no sign, what do you call't?

MARIA
The court;
I have lived in't a page.

GOTHRIO
Page! very pretty:
May I not be a page? I am old enough,
Well-timber 'd too, and I've a beard to carry it:
Pray you, Jet me be your page; I can swear already,
Upon your pantofle.

MARIA
What?

GOTHRIO
That I'll be true
Unto your smock.

MARIA
How, rascal!

OCTAVIO
Hence, and pimp
To your rams and ewes; such foul pollution is
To be whipt from court; I have now no more use of you;
Return to your trough.

GOTHRIO
Must I feed on husks,
Before I have play'd the prodigal?

OCTAVIO
No, I'll reward
Your service; live in your own element,
Like an honest man; all that is mine in the cottage,
I freely give you.

GOTHRIO
Your bottles too, that I cam'
For your own tooth!

OCTAVIO
Full as they are.

MARIA
And gold,

[Gives him her purse.

That will replenish them.

GOTHRIO
I am made for ever.
This was done i' the nick.

OCTAVIO
Why in the nick?

GOTHRIO
O sir!
'Twas well for me that you did reward my service
Before you enter'd the court; for 'tis reported
There is a drink of forgetfulness, which once tasted,
Few masters think of their servants, who, grown old,
Are turn'd off, like lame hounds and hunting horses,
To starve on the commons.

[Exit.

ALONSO
Bitter knave!

[Enter **MARTINO**.

There's craft
In the clouted shoe. Captain!

MARTINO
I am glad to kiss

Your valiant hand, and yours; but pray you, take notice,
My title's changed, I am a colonel.

PISANO
A colonel! where's your regiment?

MARTINO
Not raised yet;
All the old ones are cashier'd, and we are now
To have a new militia: all is peace here,
Yet I hold my title still, as many do
That never saw an enemy.

ALONSO
You are pleasant,
And it becomes you. Is the duke stirring?

MARTINO
Long since,
Four hours at least, but yet not ready.

PISANO
How!

MARTINO
Even so; you make a wonder oft, but leave it:

Alas, he is not now, sir, in the camp,
To be up and arm'd upon the least alarum
There's something else to be thought on: here he comes,
With his officers, new-rigg'd.

[Enter **LORENZO**, as from his chamber, with a looking-glass; **DOCTOR**, **GENTLEMAN**, and **PAGE** employed about his person.

ALONSO
A looking-glass!
Upon my head, he saw not his own face
These seven years past, but by reflection
From a bright armour.

MARTINO
Be silent, and observe.

LORENZO
So, have you done yet?
Is your building perfect?

DOCTOR
If your highness please,
Here is a water.

LORENZO
To what use? my barber
Hath wash'd my face already.

DOCTOR
But this water
Hath a strange virtue in't, beyond his art;
It is a sacred relic, part of that
Most powerful juice, with which Medea made
Old Æson young.

LORENZO
A fable! but suppose
I should give credit to it, will it work
The same effect on me?

DOCTOR
I'll undertake
This will restore the honour'd hair that grows
Upon your highness' head and chin, a little
Inclining unto gray.

LORENZO
Inclining! doctor.

DOCTOR
Pardon me, mighty sir, I went too far,
Not gray at all; I dare not flatter you
Tis something changed; but this applied will help it
To the first amber-colour, every hair
As fresh as when, your manhood in the prime,
Your grace arrived at thirty.

LORENZO
Very well.

DOCTOR
Then here's a precious oil, to which the maker
Hath not yet given a name, will soon fill up
These dimples in your face and front. I grant
They are terrible to your enemies, and set off
Your frowns with majesty; but you may please
To know, as sure you do, a smooth aspect,
Softness and sweetness, in the court of Love,

Though dumb, are the prevailing orators.

LORENZO
Will he new-create me?

DOCTOR
If you deign to taste too,
Of this confection.

LORENZO
I am in health, and need
No physic.

DOCTOR
Physic, sir! An empress,
If that an empress' lungs, sir, may be tainted
With putrefaction, would taste of it,
That night on which she were to print a kiss
Upon the lips of her long-absent lord,
Returning home with conquest.

LORENZO
'Tis predominant
Over a stinking breath, is it not, doctor?

DOCTOR
Clothe the infirmity with sweeter language:
Tis a preservative that way.

LORENZO
You are, then,
Admitted to the cabinets of great ladies,
And have the government of the borrow'd beauties
Df such as write near forty.

DOCTOR
True, my good lord,
And my attempts have prosper 'd.

LORENZO
Did you never
Minister to the princess?

DOCTOR
Sir, not yet; she's in the April of her youth, and needs not
The aids of art, my gracious lord; but in
The autumn of her age I may be useful,
And sworn her highness' doctor, and your grace

Partake of the delight.

LORENZO
Slave! witch! impostor!

[Strikes him down.

Mountebank! cheater! traitor to great nature,
In thy presumption to repair what she,
In her immutable decrees, design'd
For some few years to grow up, and then wither!
Dr is't not crime enough thus to betray
The secrets of the weaker sex, thy patients,
But thou must make the honour of this age,
And envy of the time to come, Matilda,
Whose sacred name I bow to, guilty of
A future sin in thy ill-boding thoughts,
Which for a perpetuity of youth
And pleasure she disdains to act, such is
Her purity and innocence!

[Sets his foot on the **DOCTOR'S** breast.

ALONSO
Long since
I look'd for this L'envoy.

MARTINO
Would I were well off!
He's dangerous in these humours.

OCTAVIO
Stand conceal'd.

DOCTOR
O sir, have mercy! in my thought I never
Offended you.

LORENZO
Me! most of all, thou monster!
What a mock-man property in thy intent
Wouldst thou have made me? a mere pathic to
Thy devilish art, had I given suffrage to it.
Are my gray hairs, the ornament of age,
And held a blessing by the wisest men,
And for such warranted by holy writ,
To be conceal'd, as if they were my shame?
Or plaister up these furrows in my face,

As if I were a painted bawd or whore?
By such base means if that I could ascend
To the height of all my hopes, their full fruition
Would not wipe off the scandal: no, thou wretch!
Thy cozening water and adulterate oil
I thus pour in thine eyes, and tread to dust
Thy loath'd confection with thy trumperies:
Vanish for ever!

MARTINO
You have your fee, as I take it,
Dear domine doctor! I'll be no sharer with you.

[Exit **DOCTOR**.

LORENZO
I'll court her like myself; these rich adornments
And jewels, worn by me, an absolute prince,
My order too, of which I am the sovereign,
Can meet no ill construction; yet 'tis far
From my imagination to believe
She can be taken with sublimed clay,
The silk-worm's spoils, or rich embroideries:
Nor must I borrow helps from power or greatness,
But as a loyal lover plead my cause;
If I can feelingly express my ardour,
And make her sensible of the much I suffer
In hopes and fears, and she vouchsafe to take
Compassion on me, ha! compassion?
The word sticks in my throat: what's here, that tells me
I do descend too low? rebellious spirit,
I conjure thee to leave me! there is now
No contradiction or declining left,
I must and will go on.

MARTINO
The tempest's laid;
You may present yourselves.

[**ALONZO** and **PISANO** come forward.

ALONSO
My gracious lord.

PISANO
Your humble vassal.

LORENZO

Ha! both living?

ALONSO
Sir,
We owe our lives to this good lord, and make it
Our humble suit

LORENZO
Plead for yourselves: we stand
Yet unresolved whether your knees or prayers
Can save the forfeiture of your own heads:
Though we have put our armour off, your pardon
For leaving of the camp without our license,
Is not yet sign'd. At some more fit time wait us.

[Exeunt **LORENZO**, **GENTLEMAN**, and **PAGE**.

ALONSO
How's this?

MARTINO
'Tis well it is no worse; I met with
A rougher entertainment, yet I had
Good cards to shew. He's parcel mad; you'll find him
Every hour in a several mood; this foolish love
Is such a shuttlecock! but all will be well,
When a better fit comes on him, never doubt it.

[Exeunt.

SCENE II. Another Room in the Same

Enter **GONZAGA**, **UBERTI**, **FARNEZE**, and **MANFROY**.

GONZAGA
How do you find her?

UBERTI
Thankful for my service,
And yet she gives me little hope; my rival
Is too great for me.

GONZAGA
The great duke, you mean?

UBERTI

Who else? the Milanese, although he be
A complete gentleman, I am sure despairs
More than myself.

FARNEZE
A high estate, with women,
Takes place of all desert.

UBERTI
I must stand my fortune.

[Enter **LORENZO** and **ATTENDANTS**.

MANFROY
The duke of Florence, sir.

GONZAGA
Your highness' presence
Answers my wish. Your private ear: I have used
My best persuasion, with a father's power,
To work my daughter to your ends; yet she,
Like a small bark on a tempestuous sea,
Toss'd here and there by opposite winds, resolves not
At which port to put in. This prince's merits,
Your grace and favour; nor is she unmindful
Of the brave acts (under your pardon, sir,
I needs must call them so) Hortensio
Hath done to gain her good opinion of him;
All these together tumbling in her fancy,
Do much distract her. I have spies upon her,
And am assured this instant hour she gives
Hortensio private audience; I will bring you
Where we will see and hear all.

LORENZO
You oblige me.

UBERTI
I do not like this whispering.

GONZAGA
Fear no foul play.

[Exeunt.

SCENE III. Another Room in the Same

Enter **HORTENSIO, BEATRICE**, and **TWO WAITING-WOMEN**.

1ST WOMAN
The princess, sir, long since expected you;
And, would I beg a thanks, I could tell you that
I have often moved her for you.

HORTENSIO
I am your servant.

[Enter **MATILDA**.

BEATRICE
She's come; there are others I must place to hear
The conference.

[Aside, and exit.

1ST WOMAN
Is't your excellency's pleasure
That we attend you?

MATILDA
No; wait me in the gallery.

1ST WOMAN
Would each of us, wench, had a sweetheart too
To pass away the time!

2ND WOMAN
There I join with you.

[Exeunt **WAITING-WOMEN**.

MATILDA
I fear this is the last time we shall meet.

HORTENSIO
Heaven forbid!

[Re-enter above **BEATRICE** with **LORENZO, GONZAGA, UBERTI**, and **FARNEZE**.

MATILDA
O my Hortensio!
In me behold the misery of greatness,
And that which you call beauty. Had I been
Of a more low condition, I might

Have call'd my will and faculties mine own,
Not seeing that which was to be beloved
With others' eyes: but now, ah me, most wretched
And miserable princess, in my fortune,
To be too much engaged for service done me!
It being impossible to make satisfaction
To my so many creditors; all deserving,
I can keep touch with none.

LORENZO
A sad exordium.

MATILDA
You loved me long, and without hope (alas,
I die to think on't!) Parma's prince, invited
With a too partial report of what
I was, and might be to him, left his country,
To fight in my defence. Your brave achievements
I' the war, and what you did for me, unspoken,
Because I would not force the sweetness of
Your modesty to a blush, are written here:
And, that there might be nothing wanting to
Sum up my numerous engagements, (never
In my hopes to be cancell'd.) the great duke,
Our mortal enemy, when my father's country
Lay open to his fury, and the spoil
Of the victorious army, and I brought
Into his power, hath shewn himself so noble,
So full of honour, temperance, and all virtues
That can set off a prince, that, though I cannot
Render him that respect I would, I am bound
In thankfulness to admire him.

HORTENSIO
'Tis acknowledged,
And on your part to be return 'd.

MATILDA
How can I,
Without the brand of foul ingratitude
To you, and prince Uberti?

HORTENSIO
Hear me, madam,
And what your servant shall with zeal deliver,
As a Dasdalean clew may guide you out of ,-
This labyrinth of distraction. He that loves
His mistress truly, should prefer her honour

And peace of mind, above the glutting of
His ravenous appetite: he should affect her,
But with a fit restraint, and not take from her
To give himself: he should make it the height
If his ambition, if it lie in
His stretch'd-out nerves to effect it, though she fly in
An eminent place, to add strength to her wings,
And mount her higher, though he fall himself
Into the bottomless abyss; or else
The services he offers are not real,
But counterfeit.

MATILDA
What can Hortensio
Infer from this?

HORTENSIO
That I stand bound in duty,
Though in the act I take my last farewell
Of comfort in this life,) to sit down willingly,
And move my suit no further. I confess,
Awhile you were in danger, and heaven's mercy made me
Its instrument to preserve you, (which your goodness
Prized far above the merit,) I was bold
To feed my starv'd affection with false hopes
I might be worthy of you: for know, madam,
How mean soever I appear'd in Mantua,
I had in expectation a fortune,
Though not possess'd oft, that encouraged me
With confidence to prefer my suit, and not
To fear the prince Uberti as my rival.

GONZAGA
I ever thought him more than what he seem'd.

LORENZO
Pray you, forbear.

HORTENSIO
But when the duke of Florence
Put in his plea, in my consideration
Weighing well what he is, as you must grant him
A Mars of men in arms, and, those put off,
The great example for a kingly courtier
To imitate; annex to these his wealth,
If such a large extent, as other monarchs
Call him the king of coin; and, what's above all,
His lawful love, with all the happiness

This life can fancy, from him flowing to you;
The true affection which I have ever borne you,
Does not alone command me to desist,
But, as a faithful counsellor, to advise you
To meet and welcome that felicity,
Which hastes to crown your virtues.

LORENZO
We must break off this parley:
Something I have to say.

[Exeunt above.

MATILDA
In tears I thank
Your care of my advancement; but I dare not
Follow your counsel. Shall such piety
Pass unrewarded? such a pure affection,
For any ends of mine, be undervalued?
Avert it, heaven! I will be thy Matilda,
Or cease to be; no other heat but what
Glows from thy purest flames, shall warm this bosom,
Nor Florence, nor all monarchs of the earth,.
Shall keep thee from me.

[Re-enter below **LORENZO, GONZAGA, UBERTI, FARNEZE,** and **MANFROY.**

HORTENSIO
I fear, gracious lady,
Our conference hath been overheard.

MATILDA
The better:
Your part is acted; give me leave at distance
To zany it. Sir, on my knees thus prostrate
Before your feet

LORENZO
This must not be, I shall
Both wrong myself and you in suffering it.

MATILDA
I will grow here, and weeping thus turn marble,
Unless you hear and grant the first petition,
A virgin, and a princess, ever tendered:
Nor does the suit concern poor me alone,
It hath a stronger reference to you,
And to your honour; and, if you deny it,

Both ways you suffer. Remember, sir, you were not
Born only for yourself, heaven's liberal hand
Design'd you to command a potent nation,
Gave you heroic valour, which you have
Abused, in making unjust war upon
A neighbour-prince, a Christian; while the Turk,
Whose scourge and terror you should be, securely
Wastes the Italian confines: 'tis in you
To force him to pull in his horned crescents,.
And 'tis expected from you.

LORENZO
I have been
In a dream, and now begin to wake.

MATILDA
And will you
Forbear to reap the harvest of such glories,
Now ripe, and at full growth, for the embraces
Of a slight woman? or exchange your triumphs
For chamber-pleasures, melt your able
 (That should with your victorious sword make way
Through the armies of your enemies) in loose
And wanton dalliance? be yourself, great sir,
The thunderbolt of war, and scorn to sever
Two hearts long since united; your example
May teach the prince Uberti to subscribe
To that which you allow of.

LORENZO
The same tongue
That charm 'd my sword out of my hand, and threw
A frozen numbness on my active spirit,
Hath disenchanted me. Rise, fairest princess!
And, that it may appear I do receive
Your counsel as inspired from heaven, I will
Obey and follow it: I am your debtor,
And must confess you have lent my weaken'd reason
New strengths once more to hold a full command
Over my passions. Here, to the world,
I freely do profess that I disclaim
All interest in you, and give up my title,
Such as it is, to you, sir; and, as I'ar
As I have power* thus join your hands.

GONZAGA
To yours
I add my full consent.

UBERTI
I am lost, Farneze.

FARNEZE
Much nearer to the port than you suppose:
In me our laws speak, and forbid this contract.

MATILDA
Ah me, new stops!

HORTENSIO
Shall we be ever cross'd thus?

FARNEZE
There is an act upon record, confirm'd
By your wise predecessors, that no heir
Of Mantua (as questionless the princess
Is the undoubted one) must be join'd in marriage,
But where the match may strengthen the estate
And safety of the dukedom. Now, this gentleman,
However I must style him honourable,
And of a high desert, having no power
To make this good in his alliance, stands
Excluded by our laws; whereas this prince,
Of equal merit, brings to Mantua
The power and principality of Parma:
And therefore, since the great duke hath let fall
His plea, there lives no prince that justlier can
Challenge the princess' favour.

LORENZO
Is this true, sir?

GONZAGA
I cannot contradict it.

[Enter **MANFROY**.

MANFROY
There's an ambassador
From Milan, that desires a present audience;
His business is of highest consequence,
As he affirms: I know him for a man
Of the best rank and quality.

HORTENSIO
From Milan!

GONZAGA
Admit him.

[Enter **AMBASSADOR**, and **JULIO** with a letter, which he presents on his knee to **HORTENSIO**.

How! so low?

AMBASSADOR
I am sorry, sir,
To be the bringer of this heavy news;
But since it must be known

HORTENSIO
Peace rest with him!
I shall find fitter time to mourn his loss.
My faithful servant too!

JULIO
I am o'erjoy'd,
To see your highness safe.

HORTENSIO
Pray you, peruse this,
And there you'll find that the objection,
The lord Farneze made, is fully answer'd.

GONZAGA
The great John Galeas dead!

LORENZO
And this his brother,
The absolute lord of Milan!

MATILDA
I am revived.

UBERTI
There's no contending against destiny:
I wish both happiness.

[Enter **ALONZO, MARIA, OCTAVIO, PISANO**, and **MARTINO**.

LORENZO
Married, Alonzo!
I will salute your lady, she's a fair one,
And seal your pardon on her lips.

[Kisses **MARIA**.

GONZAGA
Octavio!
Welcome e'en to my heart. Rise, I should kneel
To thee for mercy.

OCTAVIO
The poor remainder of
My age shall truly serve you.

MATILDA
You resemble
A page I had, Ascanio.

MARIA
I am
Your highness' servant still.

LORENZO
All stand amazed
At this unlook'd-for meeting; but defer
Your several stories. Fortune here hath shown
Her various power; but virtue, in the end,
Is crown'd with laurel: Love hath done his parts too;
And mutual friendship, after bloody jars,
Will cure the wounds received in our wars.

[Exeunt.

EPILOGUE

Pray you, gentlemen, keep your seats; something I would
Deliver to gain favour, if I could,
To us, and the still doubtful author. He,
When I desired an epilogue, answer d me,
"'Twas to no purpose: he must stand his fate,
Since all entreaties now would come too late;
You being long since resolved what you would say
Of him, or us, as you rise, or of the play."
A strange old fellow! yet this sullen mood
Would quickly leave him, might it be understood
You part not hence displeased. I am design d
To give him certain notice: if you find
Things worth your liking, shew it. Hope and fear,
Though different passions, have the self-same ear.

This biography was initially written in 1830

Very few materials exist for a life of Massinger beyond the entries of the Parish Register or the College Books, and a few slender intimations scattered here and there in the dedications to his plays. From these scanty sources the following brief memoir is derived.

Our author was born at Salisbury in the year 1584: he was the son of Arthur Massinger, a gentleman in the service of Henry, the second Earl of Pembroke. We must not suppose, from his being thus attached to the family of a nobleman, that the father of our poet was a person of inferior birth and station. In those days the word servant carried with it no sense of degradation. The great lords and officers of the court numbered inferior nobles among their followers. We read, in Cavendish's Life of Wolsey, that "my Lord Percy, the son and heir of the Earl of Northumberland, attended upon and was servitor to the lord-cardinal:" and from the situation which Arthur Massinger held in the household of so high and influential a person as the Earl of Pembroke, we might be justly led to argue rather favourably than unfavourably of his family and his connexions. "There were," says Mr. Gifford, "many considerations which united to render this state of dependance respectable and even honourable. The secretaries, clerks, and assistants, of various departments, were not then, as now, nominated by the government, but left to the choice of the person who held the employment; and as no particular dwelling was officially set apart for their residence, they were entertained in the house of their principal. That communication, too, between noblemen of power and trust, both of a public and private nature, which is now committed to the post, was in those days managed by confidential servants, who were despatched from one to the other, and even to the sovereign;" and, indeed, the father of our poet himself was, we know, in one instance thus employed as the bearer of communications from his patron to Elizabeth. We read in The Sidney Letters, "Mr. Massinger is newly come up from the Earl of Pembroke with letters to the queen for his lordship's leave to be away this St. George's Day." This was an errand which would not have been intrusted to the execution of any inconsiderable person: unimportant as the occasion may appear to us, it would not have been regarded in that light by Elizabeth; for no monarch ever exacted from the nobility, and particularly from her officers of state, a more rigid and scrupulous compliance with stated order than this princess.

With regard to the early youth of Massinger, we possess no information whatever. Mr. Gifford supposes that it might have been passed at Wilton, a seat belonging to the Earl of Pembroke, in the neighbourhood of Salisbury; but this mode of disposing of his early years rests on a very improbable conjecture. It may occasionally have happened that the child of a favourite dependant was admitted as the companion of the younger branches of the patron's family, and allowed to receive his education among them; but this was certainly not an ordinary case; and, like Cavendish, a large majority of the great man's servants and dependants "left wife and children, home and family, rest and quietness, only to serve him."—Massinger was most likely educated at the grammar-school of Salisbury, where many distinguished characters have received the rudiments of their education, among whom the elegant and accomplished Addison is to be numbered. But wherever the first years of our poet's life may have been spent, and whatever may have been the nature of his education, we know that at the age of eighteen (May 14, 1602) he was entered at the university of Oxford, and became a commoner of St. Alban's Hall.

Massinger resided at Oxford about four years, and then abruptly left it, without taking any degree. The cause of this sudden departure is ascribed by Mr. Gifford to the death of his father, from whom his supplies were derived: but Davies relates a very different story, and asserts that the Earl of Pembroke, who had sent him to the university and maintained him there, withdrew the necessary allowance in consequence of his having misapplied the time demanded for severer studies, in the pursuit of a more attractive but less profitable description of literature. Each opinion is equally ungrounded on the basis of any substantial evidence, and rests almost entirely on the imagination of the biographer: what slight authority there is favours the latter supposition, which, perhaps, on the whole, is most consistent with the known circumstances of the case. Anthony Wood, who was born, lived, and died at Oxford; who spent his time in collecting and recording the gossip which circulated in the university respecting the characters and conduct of its more distinguished sons; and whose evidence, however indifferent it may be, is the best that can be obtained upon the subject, confirms the representation of Davies:— "Massinger," says Wood, "gave his mind more to poetry and romance, for about four years or more, than to logic and philosophy, which he ought to have done, as he was patronised to that end." This passage corroborates the account of Davies so far as to intimate that patronage was afforded to our author, and that cause of dissatisfaction was given to the patron; but it goes no farther: it does not even state to whom the poet was indebted for assistance, nor that the misapplication of his academic hours was at all resented by the friend from whom the assistance was received: but still Wood is very probably correct in his information that other than his paternal funds were depended upon for maintaining Massinger at the university; and if such was the case, there can be no question from whose hands they must have proceeded; while the simple fact of his having been totally neglected, from the time of his father's death, by the whole of the Pembroke family, till after the demise of the earl, carries with it a strong suspicion that some offence was committed on the side of the poet, and tenaciously remembered on the side of the peer. Henry, the second Earl of Pembroke, died (1601) the year before Massinger was admitted at Oxford; and William, the third earl, to whom the father of Massinger continued attached during life, is universally and justly considered one of the brightest ornaments of the courts of Elizabeth and James. He was a man of generous and liberal disposition; the distinguished patron of arts and learning; and a lover of poetry, which he himself cultivated with some degree of success. It is not probable—it is impossible—that such a man should have allowed the highly talented son of an old and faithful servant of his family to be checked in his course of study, and abandoned to maintain, through the early years of life, a single-handed contest with adversity, for the want of that pecuniary aid which he could have yielded and never missed, unless some strong and decided cause of displeasure had existed. Had Massinger been merely forced to leave the university, as Mr. Gifford supposes, because the funds necessary to maintain him there had failed with the life of his father, we impute an act of illiberality to the Earl of Pembroke which is inconsistent with the whole tenor of his life and character. From whatever source the expenses of our author's education were originally defrayed, their suddenly ceasing argues in favour of the account intimated by Wood and detailed by Davies. If his father had, during his life, supported him at the university, there must have been some reason for the earl's not continuing that support when the father of Massinger was no more; and perhaps the most honourable supposition for both parties is that which represents the earl as offended by the bent of our author's studies and pursuits. By adopting this view of the case we are saved from the painful necessity of either assuming, on the one hand, that a nobleman distinguished among the most amiable characters of his age allowed a highly gifted and meritorious young man, a natural dependant of his house, to languish in the want of that countenance and protection on which he had an hereditary claim; or, on the other hand, that Massinger had incurred the displeasure of his natural and hereditary patron by the commission of some more crying offence.

Every, even the slightest, surmise of Mr. Gifford is deserving attention and respect; but I cannot admit the supposition by which he would account for the alienation that subsisted between the Earl of Pembroke and our author. That distinguished critic has inferred, from the religious sentiments contained in The Virgin Martyr, that Massinger was a Roman catholic, and for that cause neglected by the protector of his father. But if the intimations scattered through this play and others should be received as sufficient evidence of the faith of Massinger, we must, on similar evidence—the intimations contained in Measure for Measure, for instance—conclude that the religion of Shakspeare was the same; and then we are cast back upon our old difficulty, and have to explain why William Earl of Pembroke, a celebrated patron of literary men, and of dramatists in particular, scorned to yield his notice to the catholic Massinger, while (to use the expression of Heminge and Condell) he "prosequuted" the catholic Shakspeare and "his works with so much favour?" There are many reasons for believing Shakspeare to have been a member of the church of Rome; and the patronage afforded him by the Earl of Pembroke proves, that that nobleman extended his liberality to men of genius without any regard to distinctions of faith; but, on the other hand, we have no just grounds for assuming that Massinger really did hold the same opinions. The only evidence we have upon this point, that afforded by the general tone of his writings, is of a most vague and superficial description. What, in fact, can be inferred from it? We may from such a source derive very satisfactory information respecting the sentiments which would be favourably received by the audience, but very little respecting those of the author. The truth is, that though the national religion was reformed in its liturgy and articles, the feelings, prejudices, and superstitions of the people were still almost entirely catholic; and Massinger, like any other dramatic author, writing for the amusement of the people, necessarily addressed them in a language they would understand, and with sentiments that accorded with their own. Besides, as a poet, he would never carry his theological distinctions to his literary labours: Voltaire himself is catholic in his tragedies; and Massinger naturally adopted the creed which was most suitable to the purposes of poetry, and afforded the most picturesque ceremonies and romantic situations. I feel inclined, therefore, to dismiss entirely the theory suggested by Mr. Gifford, for these two reasons; first, supposing our author to have been a catholic, we have no reason for condemning the Earl of Pembroke as a bigot and a persecutor, who would close his eyes to the merits of so great an author, because his faith did not tally with his own; and, secondly, we have no sufficient grounds for supposing him to have been a catholic at all. But with regard to all such visionary conjectures, thinking is literally a waste of thought.

Whatever may have been the nature of Massinger's studies at Oxford, it is quite certain, from the general character of his works, that his time could not have been wasted there; and his literary acquirements, at the period of his leaving the university, appear to have been multifarious and extensive. He was about two-and-twenty (1606) when he arrived in London, where, as he more than once observes, he was driven by his necessities, and somewhat inclined, perhaps, by the peculiar bent of his talents, to dedicate himself to the service of the stage.

The theatre, when Massinger first took up his abode in the metropolis, must have presented attractions of all others the most calculated to excite the interest, and inspire the imagination, of a young man of sensibility, taste, and education like our poet. No art ever attained a more rapid maturity than the dramatic art in England. The people had, indeed, been long accustomed to a species of exhibition, called MIRACLES or MYSTERIES, founded on sacred subjects, and performed by the ministers of religion themselves, on the holy festivals, in or near the churches, and designed to instruct the ignorant in the leading facts of sacred history. From the occasional introduction of allegorical characters, such as Faith, Death, Hope, or Sin, into these religious dramas, representations of another kind, called MORALITIES, had by degrees arisen, of which the plots were more artificial, regular, and connected, and which were entirely formed of such personifications: but the first rough draught of a regular tragedy and comedy—Lord Sackville's Gorboduc, and Still's Gammer Gurton's Needle—were not produced till within the latter half of the sixteenth century, and little more than twenty years before the stage acquired its highest splendour in the productions of Shakspeare.

About the end of the sixteenth century, the attention of the public began to be more generally directed to the drama; and it throve most admirably beneath the cheering beams of popular favour. The theatrical performances which in the early part of Elizabeth's reign had been exhibited on temporary stages, erected in such halls or apartments as the actors could procure, or, more generally, in the yards of the larger inns, while the spectators surveyed them from the surrounding windows and galleries, began to find more convenient and permanent habitations. About the year 1569, a regular playhouse, under the appropriate name of The Theatre, was erected. It is supposed to have stood somewhere in Blackfriars; and, three years after the commencement of this establishment, the queen, yielding to her own inclination for such amusements, and disregarding the remonstrances of the Puritans, granted licence and authority to the servants of the Earl of Leicester ("for the recreation of her loving subjects, as for her own solace and pleasure when she should think good to see them") to exercise their occupation throughout the whole realm of England. From this time the number of theatres increased with the increasing demands of the people. Various noblemen had their respective companies of performers, who were associated as their servants, and acted under their protection; and when Massinger left Oxford, and commenced dramatic author, there were no less than seven principal theatres open in the metropolis.

With respect to the interior arrangements, there were very few points of difference between our modern theatres and those of the days of Massinger. The prices of admission, indeed, were considerably cheaper: to the boxes the entrance was a shilling; to the pit and galleries only sixpence. Sixpence also was the price paid for stools upon the stage; and these seats, as we learn from Decker's Gull's Hornbook, were particularly affected by the wits and critics of the time. The conduct of the audience was less restrained by the sense of public decorum, and smoking tobacco, playing at cards, eating and drinking, were generally prevalent among them. The hours of performance were also earlier: the play commencing at one o'clock. During the representation a flag was unfurled at the top of the theatre; and the stage, according to the universal practice of the age, was strewn with rushes; but, in all other respects, the theatres of Elizabeth and James's days seem to have borne a perfect resemblance to our own. They had their pit, where the inferior class of spectators, the groundlings, vented their clamorous censure or approbation; they had their boxes—rooms as they were called—to which the right of exclusive admission was engaged by the night, for the more affluent portion of the audience; and there were again the galleries, or scaffoldings above the boxes, for those who were content to purchase less commodious situations at a cheaper rate. On the stage, in the same manner, the appointments appear to have been nearly of the same description as at present. The curtain divided the audience from the actors, which, at the third sounding, not indeed of the bell, but of the trumpet, was drawn for the commencement of the performance. Malone, in his account of the ancient theatre, supposes that there were no moveable scenes; that a permanent elevation of about nine feet was raised at the back of the stage, from which, in many of the old plays, part of the dialogue was spoken; and that there was a private box on each side this platform. Such an arrangement would have destroyed all theatrical illusion; and it seems extraordinary that any spectators should desire to fix themselves in a station where they could have seen nothing but the backs and trains of the performers; but, as Malone himself acknowledges the spot to have been inconvenient, and that "it is not very easy to ascertain the precise situation where these boxes really were", it may very reasonably be presumed, that they were not placed in the position that the historian of the English stage has supposed. As to the permanent floor, or upper stage, of which he speaks, he may or may not be correct in his statement. All that his quotations upon the subject really establish is, that in the old, as in the modern theatre, when the actor was to speak from a window, or balcony, or the walls of a fortress, the requisite ingenuity was not wanting to contrive a representation of the place. But with regard to the use of painted moveable scenery, it is not possible, from the very circumstances of the case, to believe him correct in his theory. Such a contrivance could not have escaped our ancestors. All the materials were ready to their hands. They had not to invent for themselves, but merely to adapt an old invention to that peculiar purpose; and at a time when every better-furnished apartment was adorned with tapestry; when even the rooms of the commonest taverns were hung with painted cloths; while all the materials were constantly before their eyes, we can hardly believe our forefathers to have been so deficient in ingenuity, as to have missed the simple contrivance of converting the common ornaments of their walls into the decorations of their theatres. But, in fact, the use of scenery was almost co-existent with the introduction of dramatic representations in this country. In the Chester Mysteries (1268), the most ancient and complete collection of the kind which we possess, is found the following stage direction: "Then Noe shall go into the arke with all his familye, his wife excepte. The arke must be boarded round about; and upon the boardes all the beastes and fowles, hereafter rehearsed, must be painted, that their wordes may agree with their pictures." In this passage we have a clear reference to a painted scene. It is not likely that, in the lapse of three centuries, while all other arts were in a state of rapid improvement, and the art of dramatic writing, perhaps, more rapidly and successfully improved than any other, the art of theatrical decoration should have alone stood still. It is not improbable that their scenes were few; and that they were varied, as occasion might require, by the introduction of different pieces of stage furniture. Mr. Gifford, who adheres to the opinions of Malone, says, "A table with a pen and ink thrust in, signified that the stage was a counting-house; if these were withdrawn and two stools put in their place, it was then a tavern." And this might be perfectly satisfactory as long as the business of the play was supposed to be passing within doors; but when it was removed to the open air, such meagre devices would no longer be sufficient to guide the imagination of the audience, and some new method must have been adopted to indicate the place of action. After giving the subject very considerable attention, I cannot help thinking that Steevens was right in rejecting Malone's theory, and concluding that the spectators were, as at the present day, assisted in following the progress of the story by means of painted moveable scenery. This opinion is confirmed by the ancient stage directions. In the folio Shakspeare, 1623, we read "Enter Brutus in his orchard; Enter Timon in the woods; Enter Timon from the cave." In Coriolanus, "Marcius follows them to the gates and is shut in." Innumerable instances of the same kind might be cited to prove that the ancient stage was not so defective in the necessary decorations as some antiquaries would represent. "It may be added," says Steevens, "that the dialogue of our old dramatists has such perpetual reference to objects supposed visible to the audience, that the want of scenery could not have failed to render many of the descriptions absurd. Banquo examines the outside of Inverness castle with such minuteness, that he distinguishes even the nests which the martens had built under the projecting part of its roof. Romeo, standing in a garden, points to the tops of fruit-trees gilded by the moon. The prologue speaker to the second part of Henry the Fourth expressly shows the spectators 'This worm-eaten hold of ragged stone,' in which Northumberland was lodged. Iachimo takes the most exact inventory of every article in Imogen's bed-chamber, from the silk and silver of which her tapestry was wrought, down to the Cupids that support her andirons. Had not the inside of the apartment, with its proper furniture, been represented, how ridiculous must the action of Iachimo have appeared! He must have stood looking out of the room for the particulars supposed to be visible within it." The works of Massinger would afford innumerable instances of a similar kind to vindicate the opinion which Steevens has asserted on the testimony of Shakspeare alone. But on this subject there is one passage which appears to me quite conclusive. Must not all the humour of the mock play in The Midsummer Night's Dream have been entirely lost, unless the audience before whom it was performed were accustomed to all the embellishments requisite to give effect to a dramatic representation, and could consequently estimate the absurdity of those shallow contrivances and mean substitutes for scenery devised by the ignorance of the clowns?

In only one respect do I perceive any material difference between the mode of representation at the time of Massinger and at present: in his day, the female parts were performed by boys. This custom, which must in many cases have materially injured the illusion of the scene, was in others of considerable advantage: it furnished the stage with a succession of youths, regularly educated for the art, to fill, in every department of the drama, the characters suited to their age. When the lad had become too tall for Juliet, he had acquired the skill, and was most admirably fitted, both in age and appearance, for performing the part which Garrick considered the most difficult on the stage, because it needed "an old head upon young shoulders," the ardent and arduous character of Romeo. When the voice had "the mannish crack," that rendered the youth unfit to appear as the representative of the gentle Imogen, the stage possessed in him the very person that was wanting to do justice to the princely sentiments of Arviragus or Guiderius.

Such was the state of the stage when Massinger arrived in the metropolis, and dedicated his talents to its service. He joined a splendid fraternity, for Shakspeare, Jonson, Beaumont, Fletcher, Shirley, were then flourishing at the height of their reputation, and the full vigour of their genius. Massinger came among them no unworthy competitor for such honours and emoluments as the theatre could afford. Of the honours, indeed, he seems to have reaped a very fair and equitable portion; of the emoluments, the harvest was less abundant. In those days, very little pecuniary reward was to be gained by the dramatic poet, unless, as indeed was most frequently the case, he added the profession of the actor to that of the author, and recited the verses which he wrote. The distinguished performers of that time, Alleyn, Burbage, Heminge, Condell, Shakspeare, all appear to have died in independent, if not affluent, circumstances; but the remuneration obtained by the poet was most miserably curtailed. The price given at the theatre for a new play fluctuated between ten and twenty pounds; the copyright, if the piece was printed, might produce from six to ten pounds more; in addition to these sums, the dedication-fee may be reckoned, the usual amount of which was forty shillings. Our author appears to have produced about two or three plays every year. Most of them were successful; but, even with this industry and good fortune, his annual income would rarely have exceeded fifty pounds: and we cannot, therefore, feel surprised at finding him continually speaking of his necessities; or that the only existing document connected with his life should be one that represents him in a state of pecuniary embarrassment.

Among the papers of Dulwich College, the indefatigable Mr. Malone discovered the following letter tripartite, which, coming from persons of such deserved celebrity, cannot fail of interesting the reader.

"To our most loving friend, Mr. Phillip Hinchlow, esquire, these.

"Mr. Hinchlow,

"You understand our unfortunate extremitie, and I doe not thincke you so void of Christianitie but that you would throw so much money into the Thames as wee request now of you, rather than endanger so many innocent lives. You know there is xl. more, at least, to be receaved of you for the play. We desire you to lend us vl. of that, which shall be allowed to you; without which, we cannot be bayled, nor I play any more till this be dispatch'd. It will lose you xxl. ere the end of the next weeke, besides the hindrance of the next new play. Pray, sir, consider our cases with humanity, and now give us cause to acknowledge you our true freind in time of neede. Wee have entreated Mr. Davison to deliver this note, as well to witness your love as our promises, and alwayes acknowledgement to be ever

"Your most thankfull and loving friends,
"NAT. FIELD."

"The money shall be abated out of the money remayns for the play of Mr. Fletcher and ours.
"ROB. DABORNE."

"I have ever found you a true loving friend to mee, and in soe small a suite, it beinge honest, I hope you will not fail us.
"PHILIP MASSINGER."

Indorsed.
"Received by mee, Robert Davison, of Mr. Hinchlow, for the use of Mr. Daboerne, Mr. Feeld, Mr. Messenger, the sum of vl.
"ROB. DAVISON."

The occasion of the distress in which these three distinguished persons were involved it is not possible to fathom. We may imagine a thousand emergencies, either creditable or discreditable to the fame of the writers, with which the letter would perfectly tally; but, on such slight and vague intimations, no ingenuity could determine which was most likely to be correct. But from the document a circumstance is ascertained, which, before its discovery, had been called in question. Sir Aston Cockayne, a friend of Massinger, had asserted in a volume of poems, published in 1658, that our author had written in conjunction with Fletcher; Davies doubted this report, but the above letter establishes the fact beyond the possibility of dispute.

Massinger is known to have produced thirty-seven plays for the stage, a list of which is given at the conclusion of this memoir. Sixteen entire plays and the fragment of another, The Parliament of Love, alone are extant. No less than eleven of his productions, in manuscript, were in possession of Mr. Warburton (Somerset Herald), and destroyed with the rest of that gentleman's invaluable collection by his cook, who, ignorant of their worth, used them as waste paper for the purposes of the kitchen.

The great and various merits of the works of Massinger will be better seen in the following volumes than in any elaborate, critical dissertation. If our author be compared with the other dramatic writers of his age, we cannot long hesitate where to place him. More natural in his characters and more poetical in his diction than Jonson or Cartwright, more elevated and nervous than Fletcher, the only writers who can be supposed to contest his pre-eminence, Massinger ranks immediately under Shakspeare himself. Our poet excels, perhaps, more in the description than in the expression of passion; this may in some measure be ascribed to his attention to the fable: while his scenes are managed with consummate skill, the lighter shades of character and sentiment are lost in the tendency of each part to the catastrophe. The melody, force, and variety of his versification are always remarkable. The prevailing beauties of his productions are dignity and elegance; their predominant fault is want of passion.

Massinger's last play—which is unfortunately lost—The Anchoress of Pausilippo, was acted Jan. 26, 1640, about six weeks before his death, which happened on the 17th of March, 1640. He went to bed in good health, says Langbaine, and was found dead in the morning, in his own house on the Bankside. He was buried in the churchyard of St. Saviour's, and the comedians paid the last sad duty to his name, by attending him to the grave.

It does not appear, though every stone and every fragment of a stone has been carefully examined, that any monument or inscription of any kind marked the place where his dust was deposited. "The memorial of his mortality," says Gifford, "is given with a pathetic brevity, which accords but too well with the obscure and humble passages of his life: March 20, 1639-40, buried Philip Massinger, A STRANGER."

Such is all the information that remains to us of this distinguished poet. But though we are ignorant of every circumstance respecting him but that he lived, wrote, and died, we may yet form some idea of his personal character from the recommendatory poems prefixed to his several plays, in which, as Mr. Gifford justly observes, the language of his panegyrists, though warm, expresses an attachment apparently derived not so much from his talents as his virtues: he is their beloved, much-esteemed, dear, worthy, deserving, honoured, long-known, and long-loved friend. All the writers of his life represent him as a man of singular modesty, gentleness, candour, and affability; nor does it appear that he ever made or found an enemy.

PHILIP MASSINGER – A CONCISE BIBLIOGRAPHY

As would be expected many works from this time no longer exist either in part or their entirety. Further many playwrights collaborated on plays or revised them for later performances and we have used the latest position known on each of them for the bibliography below.

Solo Plays
The Maid of Honour, tragicomedy (c. 1621; printed 1632)
The Duke of Milan, tragedy (c. 1621–3; printed 1623, 1638)
The Unnatural Combat, tragedy (c. 1621–6; printed 1639)
The Bondman, tragicomedy (licensed 3 December 1623; printed 1624)
The Renegado, tragicomedy (licensed 17 April 1624; printed 1630)
The Parliament of Love, comedy (licensed 3 November 1624; MS)
A New Way to Pay Old Debts, comedy (c. 1625; printed 1632)
The Roman Actor, tragedy (licensed 11 October 1626; printed 1629)
The Great Duke of Florence, tragicomedy (licensed 5 July 1627; printed 1636)
The Picture, tragicomedy (licensed 8 June 1629; printed 1630)
The Emperor of the East, tragicomedy (licensed 11 March 1631; printed 1632)
Believe as You List, tragedy (rejected by the censor in January, but licensed 6 May 1631; MS)
The City Madam, comedy (licensed 25 May 1632; printed 1658)
The Guardian, comedy (licensed 31 October 1633; printed 1655)
The Bashful Lover, tragicomedy (licensed 9 May 1636; printed 1655)

Collaborations with John Fletcher
Sir John van Olden Barnavelt, tragedy (August 1619; MS)
The Little French Lawyer, comedy (c. 1619–23; printed 1647)
A Very Woman, tragicomedy (c. 1619–22; licensed 6 June 1634; printed 1655)
The Custom of the Country, comedy (c. 1619–23; printed 1647)

The Double Marriage, tragedy (c. 1619–23; Printed 1647)
The False One, history (c. 1619–23; printed 1647)
The Prophetess, tragicomedy (licensed 14 May 1622; printed 1647)
The Sea Voyage, comedy (licensed 22 June 1622; printed 1647)
The Spanish Curate, comedy (licensed 24 October 1622; printed 1647)
The Lovers' Progress or The Wandering Lovers, tragicomedy (licensed Dec 1623; rev 1634; printed 1647)
The Elder Brother, comedy (c. 1625; printed 1637).

Collaborations with John Fletcher and Francis Beaumont
Thierry and Theodoret, tragedy (c. 1607; printed 1621)
The Coxcomb, comedy (1608–10; printed 1647)
Beggars' Bush, comedy (c. 1612–15; revised 1622; printed 1647)
Love's Cure, comedy (c. 1612–15; revised 1625; printed 1647).

Collaborations with John Fletcher and Nathan Field
The Honest Man's Fortune, tragicomedy (1613; printed 1647)
The Queen of Corinth, tragicomedy (c. 1616–18; printed 1647)
The Knight of Malta, tragicomedy (c. 1619; printed 1647).

Collaborations with Nathan Field
The Fatal Dowry, tragedy (c. 1619, printed 1632); adapted by Nicholas Rowe: The Fair Penitent

Collaborations with John Fletcher, John Ford, and William Rowley, or John Webster
The Fair Maid of the Inn, comedy (licensed 22 January 1626; printed 1647).

Collaborations with John Fletcher, Ben Jonson, and George Chapman
Rollo Duke of Normandy, or The Bloody Brother, tragedy (c. 1616–24; printed 1639).

Collaborations with Thomas Dekker
The Virgin Martyr, tragedy (licensed 6 October 1620; printed 1622).

Collaborations with Thomas Middleton and William Rowley
The Old Law, comedy (c. 1615–18; printed 1656).

www.ingramcontent.com/pod-product-compliance
Lightning Source LLC
Chambersburg PA
CBHW060121050426
42448CB00010B/1986